THEOLOGY FOR TODAY

A DISTANCE LEARNING
APPROACH TO THEOLOGY

**THE
PRIORY
INSTITUTE**

THE PRIORY INSTITUTE

The Priory Institute, established in the Dominican tradition, is a centre for education in theological and biblical studies. It offers an extensive range of seminars and programmes including a certificate, diploma and degree in theology by distance learning in association with the University of Wales, Lampeter, and a part-time degree in theology in association with HETAC and the Institute of Technology, Tallaght.

THE PRIORY INSTITUTE TEAM

Joseph Kavanagh *moderator*
John Littleton *head of distance education*
Martin Cogan *general editor*
Joseph Cullen *head of adult education*
Joan Nolan *accounts and office administrator*
Magdalena Nagler *student services administrator*

THEOLOGY FOR TODAY

Student Introduction:
　　A Distance Learning Approach to Theology

Level One: (certificate programme)

1. Introduction to Theology
2. Introduction to Scripture
3. Introduction to Philosophy
4. Introduction to Christian Spirituality

Levels Two and Three: (diploma and degree programmes)

5.	Fundamental Theology	13.	Isaiah and Biblical Prophecy
6.	Themes in Modern Philosophy	14.	Philosophical Theology
7.	The God of Christian Faith	15.	Trinity & Incarnate Word
8.	Fundamental Moral Theology	16.	Caring for Life
9.	Church History	17.	Soteriology and Eschatology
10.	Christianity and World Religions	18.	The Psalms
11.	The Gospel of Mark	19.	Church and Sacraments
12.	A Just Society?	20.	Pauline Writings

A DISTANCE LEARNING APPROACH TO THEOLOGY

Series:	Theology for Today
Title:	A Distance Learning Approach to Theology
Contents:	Section One: An Introduction to Distance Learning
	Section Two: Introducing Theology
	Section Three: Revelation and Faith

ISBN:	978-1-905193-30-1
Author:	John Littleton
Published by:	The Priory Institute
Editor:	Martin Cogan
Typesetting:	The Priory Institute
Design:	The Priory Institute
Printing:	The Leinster Leader, Naas, Co Kildare, Ireland

The Priory Institute
Tallaght Village, Dublin 24, Ireland
Telephone: (+353-1) 404 8124. Fax: (+353-1) 462 6084
email: enquiries@prioryinstitute.com　　　　Website: www.prioryinstitute.com

A DISTANCE LEARNING APPROACH TO THEOLOGY

VOLUME CONTENTS

CONTENTS

A DISTANCE LEARNING APPROACH TO THEOLOGY

A DISTANCE LEARNING APPROACH TO THEOLOGY

A DISTANCE LEARNING APPROACH TO THEOLOGY

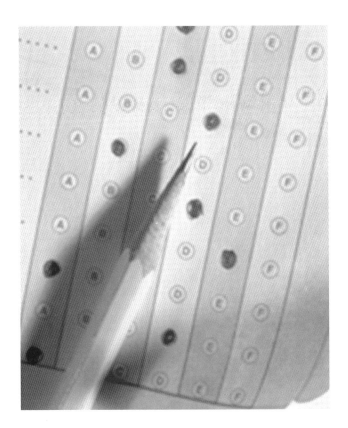

INTRODUCTION

I. THEOLOGY AND METHOD

Welcome to the study of theology, and especially to this introductory book on the distance learning approach to theology. The book has been especially designed both as an exploration of the Christian faith and as a way of understanding the methodology of distance learning.

Some students may have studied theology before. For those who have, then the modules which follow this introduction should clarify something of what is already known and introduce these students to a more comprehensive study of particular issues in theology.

This introductory book, together with the modules which follow, should stimulate an interest in theology to such an extent that it may become a lifelong activity. Any study of theology deepens one's faith and broadens one's commitment.

Theology is a fascinating subject to study. However, before beginning to study theology properly, some time is needed to reflect on the distinctive methodology being used – the distance learning approach. Firstly, some of the techniques of this approach will be introduced and, secondly, an appreciation of theology as a worthwhile topic will be developed.

Therefore, this book is divided into three sections.

a)   Section One provides an introduction to distance learning, along with an outline of the central components of the distance learning approach to contemporary education;

b)   Section Two focuses on how theological thinking functions for the contemporary Christian; and

c)   Section Three introduces some fundamental theological ideas, especially revelation and faith.

By the end of this book, having practised some of the required techniques, students will have an initial understanding of what theology is about. It will then be possible to proceed to the main modules in the Priory Institute's theology programme.

The study of theology may also help students to know and understand God more fully and, as a result, to deepen their personal relationship with God leading to a stronger appreciation of the presence of God in the Church, in all people and in the whole world.

EXERCISE 1:

a)   Using an exercise book, or a computer, write a short paragraph expressing why you enrolled for a particular module in this programme and what you want to achieve from studying the module?

b)   As you begin this book, what are your hopes and expectations? List 3 of them.

c)   What are your anxieties as you begin this distance learning venture? List 3 of them.

In the course of this introduction, students will be asked to return to these answers occasionally in order to draw attention to the development of their hopes, expectations and fears as they progress through the various sections. As the introduction continues, students will become more accustomed to the instructive and interactive methods of distance education which includes both teaching and learning.

1.1   THE IMPORTANCE OF EXERCISES

The exercises throughout this book – and, indeed, throughout all modules in the programme – are an *invaluable* and *essential* part of the learning process. It is very important that students complete *all* the exercises as they progress through the book. These will test the students' understanding of the reading material and challenge them to make connections between what they have read and the situations of their own lives. The act of writing is an integral part of the distance learning technique, and without it the method does not work properly. Students who use a word processor should retain all their files in an orderly fashion. Students who are hand-writing their exercises should maintain an orderly and complete exercise book. Be sure to date all written material. Occasionally lecturers or academic tutors may wish to discuss the students' written work with them and to enquire as to how well they are progressing and in what way their work could be enhanced. Remember, even if students find some of the exercises very easy, these should not be skipped. The process of accurately formulating and writing correct answers is a vital part of the distance learning method.

The act of writing is an integral part of the distance learning technique, and without it the method does not work properly.

The process of accurately formulating and writing correct answers is a vital part of the distance learning method.

SECTION ONE:
AN INTRODUCTION TO DISTANCE LEARNING

I.   STARTING AT THE BEGINNING

I.I   OBJECTIVES OF THIS SECTION

Once this section has been completed, students should be able:

a)   to understand the concept of distance learning and be familiar with the main principles being used. Students should also be able to assess themselves on the written exercises which have been completed during the section;

b)   to use the required reading and other source material appropriately. Students will be able to assess their understanding of the material by their ability to use it correctly in written work;

c)   to grasp how the process of writing facilitates the logical expression of ideas. Again, students will be able to assess this from the written exercises that have been completed.

Each unit has its own aims and objectives, so students must be clear on the differences between *aims* and *objectives*.

- Aims are expressed in general terms and are aspirational. Their attainment cannot necessarily be proven. For example, one of the aims of this section is that, because of the reading and reflection undertaken, the student's spiritual life will be deepened. Obviously, this cannot be objectively proven.

- In contrast, objectives can be tested empirically. In other words, students must be able to demonstrate that they have achieved their objectives. For example, one of the objectives of this section is that students will be able to demonstrate just how much their written exercises have facilitated the logical expression of ideas. When assessing any written work, it will be possible to verify whether or not this objective has been achieved.

2. DISTANCE LEARNING AND LIFELONG EDUCATION

2.1 THE REALITY OF LIFELONG LEARNING

People often imagine that learning has ceased once they have completed their formal school or college education. However, in reality, we spend our whole life in learning situations that deepen our understanding of ourselves and the world around us. We learn from our conversations with others, and we learn from reading newspapers and watching television. Learning is part of our natural make-up; it is part of life; it is a lifelong process.

EXERCISE 2:

a) Can you recall 3 conversations you have had during the past month that have increased your knowledge or understanding?

b) Can you list 3 new skills you have acquired during the past year?

Nowadays, there is great emphasis being placed on lifelong learning and we must be aware that such learning takes many different forms. It may take the form of continuous professional development (often abbreviated cpd) that is associated with one's employment – for example, in-service training at work. Or it may take the form of continuing education at an academic level designed to gain an extra qualification – for example, a postgraduate degree in a subject in which a person is already qualified. It may take the form of second-chance education for those who are returning to education having previously been unable, for whatever reason, to complete their normal second-level education. This may take the form, for example, of a course in basic literacy and numeracy skills, or it may be something more advanced, for example, a course in computer literacy.

Learning about God and about our religion is also a part of the everyday learning process. It often occurs during normal *conversations* with our family or neighbours. It especially happens during times of illness or bereavement when we spend extra hours reflecting on the mystery of life. It may occur when we listen to sermons in church, and it may occur when we pray.

EXERCISE 3:

a) Are you involved in any form of lifelong learning at present? If you are, write a description of it in 5 lines.

2.2 LIFELONG LEARNING AND ADULT EDUCATION

Lifelong learning may also take the form of participation in adult education programmes studied purely for personal fulfilment; for example, woodwork classes, language courses or creative art classes. Students may have enrolled for this theology programme because they are interested in exploring aspects of their faith, and hopefully they will find fulfilment in discussing with others how God impinges on their own lives and on the life of the world.

EXERCISE 4:

a) List any adult education programmes or courses that you have attended during the past two years.

Whatever the reason for students enrolling at The Priory Institute, and whatever form of lifelong learning is happening for students at this time, they are – like so many other adults – engaged in lifelong learning.

2.3   WHAT IS DISTANCE LEARNING?

Education happens in a variety of ways. Traditionally, education has been perceived as the task of a student who is enrolled in either a full-time or a part-time study programme. All of us know students who are engaged in such full-time education – students who are not expected to do any other form of work because they devote most of their time to learning (even though some full-time students need to work part-time to support themselves). Many of us also know students who are involved in part-time educational programmes. They combine their studies with full-time employment which itself requires a considerable amount of time and personal discipline in its own right. Think about yourself for a moment. Because you are combining your studies with other responsibilities, you are considered a part-time student enrolled for this theology programme.

EXERCISE 5:

a) What, in your opinion, are the advantages and disadvantages of both full-time and part-time education? Write down 3 advantages and 3 disadvantages of each.

2.4   A SEPARATE SPACE

In doing this programme, students are still somewhat different from the normal part-time student; they are engaged in *distance* learning. Simply expressed, distance learning is learning at a distance – that is obvious enough. According to A. Kaye, a renowned promoter of distance learning:

> Distance education, in contrast to traditional classroom or campus based education, is characterised by a clear separation in space and time of the majority of teaching and learning activities. Teaching is to a large degree mediated through various technologies (print, audio, video, broadcasting, internet, etc.), and learning generally takes place on an individual basis through supported independent study in the student's home or workplace.
>
> (Kaye, A.: 'Computer-Mediated Communication in Distance Education', in Mason R. and Kaye A. (eds), *Mindweave – Communication, Computers and Distance Education*, 1989, Oxford, Pergamon, p.6.)

EXERCISE 6:

a) *Think about the description of distance learning you have just read. Does this description correspond closely with your own current understanding of distance learning? Write 5 lines expressing your thoughts on what is specific about distance learning.*

2.5 THE LONELINESS OF THE LONG DISTANCE LEARNER

In the traditional approach to education, the teacher and the students are in the same place at the same time, so the learning and the teaching occur simultaneously and in the same space. Communication between the teacher and the student is personal and face-to-face.

In contrast to this, the distance learning student has very little or even no formal attendance at lectures. The teaching and the learning occur *separately* because the teacher and the students are not usually together in the same place – even though there are face-to-face encounters with coordinators, lecturers and academic tutors at study days and tutorial days.

The normal means of communication between teacher and student in distance learning is by the written word, by broadcasting or by electronic means. Also, in distance learning, students usually study alone – very often at home – using specially prepared texts and materials. Neither the teacher nor the other students are present. Distance learning students are often described in information technology jargon as being in a 'virtual classroom' or as attending a 'virtual university'.

At times, some students may feel their isolation from other students. When their study is problematic, students may wonder how the other students are progressing. Students might well imagine that others are not having the same difficulties as they are having, and as a result they may be tempted to abandon their studies. This should not dishearten any student. Although they do not attend regular classes and do not meet their teachers or fellow students every day, they do, in addition to the specially prepared texts and books, have various forms of learner support provided throughout their studies.

At the Priory Institute students have the support of a local coordinator. They also have access to a discussion forum on the Institute's website (www.prioryinstitute.com) and they have email access to an academic tutor. They have the opportunity to meet their coordinators and fellow students at study days which are organised regularly in a selection of the study centres – depending on the geographical distribution of students enrolled for any given module. Many of these local study centres are located in Dominican priories around the country and have small libraries for use by students of the Institute.

On study days, students are encouraged to share their thoughts and problems with their coordinators, lecturers and fellow students, and to discuss how their ideas are changing as they progress through the module. At some stage during the course of the module, students will probably have the opportunity to meet at least some of the writers of the various units which comprise each module. Students may also, if they wish, exchange telephone numbers or e-mail addresses with other students so that they can contact one another to discuss how their study is progressing.

EXERCISE 7:

a) How do you feel about studying alone? Write 5 lines that describe how you feel.

b) List three advantages and three disadvantages of studying alone.

In conclusion, distance learning requires a new way of thinking about education – a way that is radically different from the traditional approach to education. It requires a new mindset, and even a new frame of reference that breaks the old mould which has dominated formal education for far too long. And from students, it requires a degree of self-discipline.

3. THEOLOGY BY DISTANCE LEARNING

3.1 AN ASSESSMENT OF THE CHURCH'S POSITION

To some degree, the future of the Church depends on having well-educated and articulate laity. For so long, the laity did not have the possibility of studying their faith at a serious level. Consequently, they depended very much on the clergy to inform them about the Church's teaching and its application to daily living. Apart from teachers, the clergy were the only people trained to teach the faith. Once people had finished school education, the only opportunity for most believers to develop their knowledge of the Christian faith was through Sunday sermons.

In the past, the laity were not very involved in the thinking and administration of the Church. Their role was to receive what was handed down to them. Because of this role, a perception even developed that the Church consisted solely of the clergy (pope, bishops, priests and deacons) and that the laity were the passive onlookers or receptors. Some cynics even remarked that the purpose of the laity was 'to pray up, pay up and shut up!'

Since the connection between going to church on Sundays and living a Christian life during the week was not always adequately emphasised, it was easy to compartmentalise different areas of one's life. The practice of one's faith was frequently confined to church-going, where people said their prayers and engaged in devotional practices.

3.2 NEW TRENDS

Over the second half of the twentieth century, however, attitudes have changed. Nowadays, many people are no longer interested in religion. We live in an increasingly secular world. The decline in the number of people attending church services has been dramatic. Many people dismiss the Church and organised religion as something irrelevant. The existence of God is constantly questioned, especially because there is so much suffering and misery in the world. Some go so far as to say that religion is dead, and God (if God ever existed) is dead too.

Numerous people, conscious of their baptismal dignity, are again being motivated to think seriously about God and their faith.

However, this is not the complete story. Nowadays, there are also many people who appreciate the relevance – indeed the necessity – of linking belief in God with their religious practice and with all areas of their lives. Numerous people, conscious of their baptismal dignity, are again being motivated to think seriously about God and their faith. Moreover, a growing number of people are becoming committed members of their parish communities, and they actively seek some involvement in parish activities.

For them, participation in the Church's life and ministry is something worthwhile. They realise that the Church to which they belong is *their* Church as well as God's Church, and that they are as important and as needed as everyone else. But many who seek to express their faith in this way do so in the midst of the pressures of a very busy world where so many things have to be packed into a twenty-four hour day. Consequently, it is often almost impossible to find time for relaxation and reflection. And yet, the deeper questions about life – questions regarding the meaning and purpose of life – remain embedded in people's minds and hearts.

EXERCISE 8:

a) Stop and think for a few minutes about what you have read in the previous six paragraphs. Do you agree with this assessment of the Church in the modern world? Is it accurate and fair? Write 10 lines.

3.3   OPPORTUNITIES FOR ADULT FAITH DEVELOPMENT

Committed Christians, if they are to contribute meaningfully to the Church's mission, need opportunities to learn more about Christ, the Gospel and the Church's teaching. Many, although unhappy with Sunday sermons, are unable to avail of full-time or even part-time theology programmes owing to the pressures of work and the time constraints of family life and travel.

This leads us to the rationale for providing distance learning theology programmes. Wherever proper study opportunities are unavailable or inaccessible, the provision of a distance learning programme in theology at an academic level is among the best ways of enabling interested people to explore their faith. While distance learning programmes in many other subjects have been developed in Ireland during recent years, this is not the case with theology. The module that you are studying is part of the first significant attempt in this country at providing theological education through the mode of distance learning.

EXERCISE 9:

a) *Spend a little time considering the following: if this distance learning approach to doing theology was not available to you, are there any other ways by which you could begin to study theology?*

b) *Read and consider the following three well-known and often-used quotations regarding adult faith development. In what way, if any, do they make sense to you? Write 15 lines.*

'When I was a child, I used to talk like a child, and see things as a child does, and think like a child; but now that I have become an adult, I have finished with all childish ways.' (1 Cor 13:11)

'I want a laity who know their faith, who enter into it, who know just where they stand, who know what they hold and what they do not. I want a laity who know their creed as well that they can give an account of it, and who know enough of history to defend it. I want an intelligent, well-instructed laity' (Cardinal John Henry Newman, 1801-1890 ce).

'The faith of … adults too should continually be enlightened, stimulated and renewed, so that it may pervade the temporal realities in their charge. Thus, for Catechesis to be effective, it must be permanent, and it would be quite useless if it stopped short at the threshold of maturity, since Catechesis, admittedly under another form, proves no less necessary for adults' (Pope John Paul II, 1920-2005 ce).

c) *If you agree with the sentiments of these quotations, express in 5 lines your own vision of adult faith formation.*

NB: If you do not understand any of the technical terms, consult the glossary at the end of this book.

4.   LEARNING AS AN ADULT

4.1   THE COMPONENTS OF LEARNING

Learning is a process rather than an isolated event and, as such, has several different stages. Three key stages in the learning process are *comprehension*, *accommodation* and *application*. *Comprehension* involves the initial exposure to, and understanding of, a new idea or concept. *Accommodation* refers to the process of matching this new information within one's existing understanding of a subject – together with the possibility that, with this fresh understanding, one might need to review one's current beliefs. *Application* involves using one's new ideas in differing contexts, perhaps in problem-solving or in evaluation.

4.2   LEARNING AS AN ADULT

There is a considerable difference between learning as a child in school and learning as an adult. All adults bring the accumulated wealth of their life experiences to their new learning situations. We often hear reference to people who have been 'through the university of life', even though they may never have formally attended any lectures in higher education. In place of formal education, these are people who have accumulated much wisdom over many years. The fact is that, as adults, we continually acquire an ever-broader range of knowledge that helps us in almost all new situations. This is because we already have an existing, extensive framework of words and ideas that provide an appropriate context for assimilating any new ideas that we might discover. It is often claimed that there are teachable moments and unteachable moments in our lives – with many of the teachable moments occurring in adult life. This is especially true when we begin to study religion and engage in theological enquiry.

4.3   LEARNING ABOUT GOD AND RELIGION

Everything we already know about God and the manner in which we experience God becomes the fundamental context into which all our new ideas about God will fit. Some of these new ideas may challenge our existing ones, even to the point of demanding that we radically modify our image of God and our understanding of how God interacts with us and with the earth. Such challenges may be stimulating and reassuring. Equally, however, they may cause distress because they prompt us to question what we had previously taken for granted.

It is important to remember that adults have a wealth of experience to bring to new learning situations. Some adults imagine they are disadvantaged regarding study when compared to younger people. While adults may not have the time for study that younger people have, they have much more experience in selecting what is important from among the details – a skill which is essential in a distance learning study programme.

EXERCISE 10:

a) *Reflect on the particular wealth of experience that you, as an adult, bring to this new learning situation. Write 5 lines outlining how you believe that your life experiences will enhance your study of theology.*

4.4   OUR EXPERIENCE OF LEARNING

Students who finished school many years ago and have not formally studied anything since may feel overwhelmed at the task of reading text-books and  writing essays again. For many, the notion that 'school days were the best days of my life!' might simply be false. Study may have been difficult and some students may have had more than one experience of failure. It is, therefore, quite natural for students to have some anxiety about what is being undertaken. Remember, however, that there are many more such students who have also enrolled for this programme. No student should ever feel alone

Some distance learning students will have continued their formal studies immediately after finishing school; while for others, study may be a significant part of their professional life, for example, those involved in any branch of the teaching profession. Whatever about a student's history, this programme will be the first experience of distance learning for many, and these will be unsure about the level of expectations and commitments which are involved. Again, no student is alone. There are many other students in similar positions who have enrolled for this programme, and many have the same fears.

4.5 THE FREEDOM OF LEARNING AS AN ADULT

Studying as an adult is very different from studying as a child. With children, it is the teacher who controls the learning situation, and this is necessary because children are children, deadlines must be met and the syllabi for public examinations must be completed. Also, of course, children and teenagers would often prefer not to be at school at all, so their motivation to study is often less than ideal.

Learning as an adult is much more flexible. Adult students can choose what they want to study, and when to study it. The students are in control of the learning situation. They are doing it because they themselves choose to do so. They can set their own study pace and targets within whatever parameters suit their work, family and other commitments. Some forms of adult learning, including the programmes leading to academic credit or an approved qualification at The Priory Institute, involve strict deadlines for the completion of assignments or examinations. However, those of the Institute's programmes which are not being studied for academic credit – programmes that students are completing solely for personal interest and development – are less restrictive. Therefore, all students have the freedom to decide how to organise their daily tasks such that they can devote about eight hours of study every week for each module being undertaken.

EXERCISE 11:

Think about your weekly responsibilities and tasks.

a) List them in descending order of priority.

b) Where in your list is 'studying theology'?

c) Are you content with its position on the list? Why/Why not?

4.6 SOME USEFUL ADVICE

While it is recommended that students complete each unit of each module within the allotted time-frame (a semester calendar is provided at the launch of every module), the only deadlines that are crucial are those concerning the written assignments from students registered for academic credit, those which will be assessed and graded. However, it is very important that students spend time thinking seriously about what they read and understanding it in such a manner that it can make a positive contribution to their lives. Nonetheless, this is not a license to become complacent about the exercises spread throughout the various modules.

Students should organise their time wisely. There are many opportunities for study that do not readily occur to people. For example, it may be possible to study for part of a lunch break or while travelling to work by bus or train. Be confident. The textbooks are designed in such a way that even very short sections can be studied without students losing their feel for their overall position within the book.

5. AIDS TO COMPLETING THE PROGRAMME

5.1 STRUCTURE OF THE PROGRAMME

It is important that students understand fully the *structure* of the distance leaning programmes being offered by The Priory Institute. The module now commencing has been designed to be studied either on its own or as part of an entire programme for which an academic qualification may be earned. Each *programme* consists of various *modules*, each *module* consists of several *units*, and each *unit* is subdivided into *sections*, and *sections* may have some or many numbered *parts* and *exercises*.

PROGRAMME								
MODULE			MODULE			MODULE		
UNIT	UNIT	UNIT	UNIT	UNIT	UNIT	UNIT	UNIT	UNIT
SECTION SECTION SECTION	SECTION SECTION SECTION	SECTION SECTION SECTION	SECTION SECTION SECTION	SECTION SECTION SECTION	SECTION SECTION SECTION	SECTION SECTION SECTION	SECTION SECTION SECTION	SECTION SECTION SECTION

The section currently being studied is entitled 'An Introduction to Distance Learning' which introduces students to the techniques of distance learning. Obviously, anyone who goes on to study further modules will not have to repeat this introductory book.

5.2 HIGHLIGHT SYMBOLS

Within each section, there are several numbered parts and sub-parts. In addition to this, material of special significance is highlighted using a number of different symbols:

This symbol indicates the start of an exercise.

This symbol indicates the start of a short external text.

This symbol indicates the start of a longer text from another author.

This symbol indicates the start of material of special importance.

5.3 THE EXERCISES

The purpose of the exercises which are spread throughout this book and all subsequent modules is to help students made progress in their studies. Their purpose is not to give anyone a sense of failure should they find themselves unable to complete all the parts. Anyone having difficulties can contact their on-line academic tutor, and help will be given to complete the particular exercise. Always remember that the content of each unit is designed to stimulate and motivate students' own thinking and to help them benefit as much as possible from the time being devoted to study.

Nobody can ever know everything there is to be known about any subject. In fact, the more we learn, the more we realise how much there is still to learn.

Learning is indeed a lifelong process. In a certain sense, then, there is no failure in adult learning because we learn at our own pace according to what we need to know and understand.

The structure of the programme allows students great freedom to organise their study-times. Because the study material is predominantly in self-contained packs, in addition to studying at home, students can always take the relevant book(s) with them to the local library or when they go away for a weekend.

5.4 EXTRA READING MATERIAL

While most of the reading material required for completing each module is contained in the study packs, students are also recommended to have the following:

- a good English-language dictionary;

- a Bible – preferably a study edition with student notes;

- a basic theological dictionary;

- a one-volume Bible commentary; and

- A catechism – for example, the *Catechism of the Catholic Church*.

Students may also wish to purchase those books on the supplementary reading lists which are of special interest. Advice can be sought from the programme director, academic tutor or lecturers about purchasing or sharing books that may be required for further reading.

A visit to the local library will help familiarise students with whatever information resources they have which are related to their study.

For some information about different versions and translations of the Bible, read Appendix Two.

6. INTERACTION IN DISTANCE LEARNING

6.1 INTERACTING WITH THE TEXT

It is essential that students interact (engage actively) with the text. Unless they do, they will not derive the full benefit from the distance learning method. Always remember that when students are studying this material they are not in a classroom or lecture hall. The teacher or lecturer is not physically present. In a classroom, it is normally possible to ask the teacher questions, or seek clarification from fellow students concerning the material being presented. This is not possible in distance learning, apart from the occasions when lecturers and students assemble for study days, or when the student uses the on-line tutorial assistance, or when students contact fellow students by telephone or email.

Therefore, in distance learning, the *teaching* is done primarily through the pages of the textbook being studied. Similarly the *learning* is done mainly through the pages of the same text. The text being read, with which students are interacting, is, in effect, the teacher. All students reading this text now are learning as they read – provided, of course, they are interacting with it! Always remember that the motto of the distance learner must be: Interaction! Interaction! Interaction!

In distance learning, students have more control over the learning situation.

The exercises have not been incorporated into the text just to fill space. They have been introduced as a substitute for the face-to-face communication with a teacher and other students.

Interacting with the text means doing more than simply reading one sentence after another. It involves stopping and thinking about what is being read. It means doing whatever is being asked in the exercise boxes. This is where distance learning has an advantage over other forms of education: students can stop and go back over material whenever they feel the need, whereas in a lecture hall the teacher or lecturer may well move on to fresh material before students have adequately grasped what was being said. In distance learning, however, students have more control over the learning situation.

Sometimes, doing the exercises may seem like a waste of time. However, the exercises have not been incorporated into the text just to fill space. They have been introduced as a substitute for the face-to-face communication between a teacher and students.

6.2   THE PURPOSE OF EXERCISES

The exercises encourage students to stop and do some work. In doing so, they contribute significantly to the learning process. They test the students' understanding of the reading material and challenge them to make connections between what has been read and their real-life situations. By now, some students will have already avoided doing some of the exercises in this book because they deemed them unnecessary, irrelevant or just too simple. It is very often the case that the more qualified students are, the more resistance they have to performing the repetitive written tasks. Any student who has avoided any of them should return to them now and complete them before reading any further. As students become more accustomed to the techniques of distance learning, they will come to appreciate more fully the reasons for doing *all* the exercises.

EXERCISE 12:

a) Return to any exercise you have avoided so far in this book, and complete it.

By completing the exercises as thoroughly as possible, students will be continually reviewing and evaluating their progress throughout the module.

7.   READING AND WRITING

7.1   THE IMPORTANCE OF READING

The main purpose of reading is to develop a student's thoughts. Reading also provides students with new information. But reading in itself is not useful unless students stop to think about what has been read, and to think in such a way that they fully understand what is being communicated. When students read, they must read with a definite purpose; otherwise the learning process is not being achieved. Therefore, be prepared for plenty of reading.

Regarding the books and other written resources that students will consult, there are three types:

*   required reading: this is essential reading;
*   recommended reading: this is further reading that is advised. However, although useful, it is optional; and
*   reference reading: this is reading from reference books, for example, dictionaries or encyclopaedias or specialist books that students may consult from time to time to answer specific queries.

Students need to be astute about how they read. It is not necessary to read every book or article with the same level of intensity. Depending on students' needs, they may simply scan through the contents of a book, or they may read it quickly in order to develop just an overall impression of the topic being covered. Often, however, students will be required to read a text very closely, either because they really must understand fully what is being written, or because the text has been written in a convoluted or over-abstract style. When the text itself is difficult, it is advisable to read it twice – firstly, to obtain an overview of the content and, secondly, to explore the key elements of the argument. Students should always have a dictionary nearby when reading.

7.2   THE IMPORTANCE OF WRITING

The importance of writing regularly cannot be overemphasised. Students in a classroom normally write notes as they listen to the lecture. Writing is very important in every form of study, but it is vitally important in distance learning. Before students can write, they have to assimilate what has been heard or read. Only then can the ideas be expressed in written form. The act of writing teaches students to summarise information succinctly and to express their thoughts with clarity and order.

Writing is tremendously important in distance learning. Students need to stop and think as they read. They then need to write as often as they can about what has been read. Writing helps students to think and to clarify their understanding.

7.3   TAKING NOTES

Taking notes about what is being read can absorb a significant part of students' study-time. But there are several reasons why taking notes is beneficial. Notes help students to *remember* the main arguments in the text being read. Writing these notes assists students in *thinking*. Furthermore, notes help students to prepare for written assignments. If written properly, they provide students with an *accurate and concise* account of what has been read and will, therefore, avoid the hassle of having to re-read the material all over again.

Finally, notes are a *symbol of the progress* and they provide students with an often well-needed psychological boost. The modules to be tackled after this introductory book have been carefully designed to help in the process of learning. The quotes in the margins frequently reflect the core of the material in the main text; the illustrations provide a visual guide to the text. But more important than either of these two is the blank space in the margins. This space is designed for students to write their own notes, or questions, concerning the text. Longer notes should be written in a separate exercise book, or typed into a computer if one is accessible. Such note writing is a very good form of interaction with the text. It is perfectly acceptable to write notes directly onto the textbooks – provided, of course, the books are owned by the students.

7.4 TAKING NOTES EFFECTIVELY

Taking notes, to be effective, must be done properly. Apart from the accuracy and clarity of the notes themselves, notes taken while reading a book should include all the following details:

- the author's name or authors' names (if more than one author), with the surname first, followed by the first name;

- the title of the book (or if it is an article from a journal or a collection of essays, then the title of the article in inverted commas followed by the title of the journal or collection of essays). Only the title of the publication (and subtitle) should be typed in italics;

- the edition of the book (if it is the second or subsequent edition, or a revised edition);

- the volume number or part number (for articles);

- the year of publication;

- the place of publication;

- the name of the publisher; and

- the page numbers to which reference is made.[1]

*Attention to these details at an early stage prevents much frustration at a later stage when students are preparing assignments and bibliographies (lists of the written sources from which information has been garnered, including details of authorship, year of publication, place of publication, publisher, edition, etc.) are being assembled. There is nothing as infuriating for students as having accumulated precise notes for an assignment, and only then discovering that the sources from which these notes were taken are not known. Whenever students quote directly from an author, or when key ideas from a particular writer are being used, students **must always** acknowledge the source of these ideas – the place from which the ideas were taken. If students do not acknowledge the sources of their material, they would be vulnerable to the accusation of 'plagiarism' (the taking of another person's thoughts, writings or inventions and using them as one's own). Plagiarism in an assignment will result in an automatic failure grade for that assignment; it may also lead to other disciplinary procedures. Therefore, students should be very attentive to all publication details when taking notes. You have been warned! Far from diminishing students' written work, providing references to sources adds considerably to the scholarly quality of any writing.*

Look at the bibliography at the end of this book to see examples of bibliographical references. Note the use of italics, punctuation, etc. Also, when visiting a local library, students should look at the title pages and title page versos among the books and journals and test their ability to provide accurate and comprehensive bibliographical references for a few of them.

Whenever students quote directly from an author, or when key ideas from a particular writer are being used, students must always acknowledge the source of these ideas.

Plagiarism in an assignment will result in an automatic failure grade for that assignment.

EXERCISE 13:

a) Before reading any further, examine some of the books and magazines in your home or in the local library. Look for the publication details on each of the books. Find a few examples of each of the details listed above.

1. There are several standard footnoting systems in existence. Any student who wishes to adopt an alternative system to the one outlined above is free to do so; however, the implementation of any system must be totally consistent throughout the essay or dissertation.

8. ASSIGNMENTS

8.1 THE DISCIPLINE OF WRITING

The more students write, the more logical and sequential their thought patterns will become. This fact becomes obvious to students once they begin to prepare written assignments in later modules. The discipline of expressing an understanding of any topic within a prescribed 'word-limit' teaches students to focus their thoughts accurately on the topic in hand, it disciplines their minds to be selective about what is read and helps them to make judgements about the relative importance of the various elements being read.

8.2 THE VALUE OF ASSIGNMENTS

One of the main functions of studying theology is to enable students to *express and discuss* an understanding of God, and to grasp the way in which God is acting in human life and in the world. If students wish to gain academic credit, then the written assignments, more than anything else, will help to do this.

Assignments help students to *evaluate their progress* as the modules progress. Assignments provide both students and their assessors with an indication of how well they understand the subject-matter and appreciate its practical applications. So it is very important that they preserve their written exercises in an orderly fashion for future reference or for discussion at a study day. This can be done easily by using a computer, an exercise book or any other suitable filing system.

The regular short exercises which students write are not graded by an assessor, so they do not count towards the students' final grades. Usually, several short essays and one long essay (at Level I), or two long essays (at Levels II and III) will be graded for final assessment. However, the requirements may differ between different modules and between different levels. The shorter written exercises spread throughout the text-books must always be done and retained so that there is evidence that the material is, in fact, being covered as required.

In addition to providing students with their grades, assessors are obliged to offer comments on assignments. Always remember that the purpose of written assignments is to demonstrate to the assessors the full extent of what students know, rather than what they do not know. Therefore, students should be prepared to accept their assessor's constructive criticisms in the spirit in which they are intended. When students receive an encouraging grade for an assignment, they should be content. But when disappointing results are received, students should not become disillusioned. Students should learn from the assessor's comments so that they can perform better in future assignments. Most students write at least one assignment that does not do justice to their abilities and efforts. It is important that students learn from their mistakes and disappointments. Students should proceed with hope and confidence to the next assignment. This should be their philosophy throughout the entire programme.

8.3 PROBLEMS ASSOCIATED WITH ASSIGNMENTS

One of the most serious issues regarding written assignments is the problem of getting started, and in particular of starting to write. Many students are happy to read extensively in preparation for written assignments but are reluctant to commence with the actual writing process. Inevitably this leads to frustration as the deadline approaches. Therefore, when students are working on their written assignments, they should begin writing early, well within the time-span allowed. Preliminary drafts can easily be revised once students discover more relevant reading material later on. But a draft is needed before one can revise!

A draft is needed before one can revise!

Many students have a basic problem regarding written assignments: they do not set themselves a proper time-plan. It is essential to have a definite plan for written assignments. The lecturers and academic tutors will discuss assignment plans during the study days and tutorial days. A key part of the plan is to have the assignment properly structured. All assignments must have an introduction and a conclusion. In between the introduction and conclusion, as the various arguments are formulated, there must be ample evidence of having read widely and reflected on what has been read. There must be evidence of thorough analysis and progression of thought.

When students are writing assignments, they should always link their paragraphs using suitable link words and phrases. When offering an individual opinion, students should ensure that it is based on relevant reading and genuine reflection. Finally, students should devote attention to presentation, grammar and punctuation. Always leave wide margins so that assessors can insert their comments. Consult the 'guidelines for written assignments' that form part of the study pack given to students at the launch of the various modules.

8.4 THE ROLE OF ACADEMIC TUTORS

It is most important to realise that the academic tutor's main role is to help students complete the units and modules successfully. The tutors are provided to help and encourage students achieve their full learning potential.

Tutors are not examiners; they will monitor the students' progress and will advise them about their reading.

Tutors are not examiners; they will monitor the students' progress, advise them about their reading and offer advice to any student who has a mental block about a particular assignment. The tutors accompany students as they proceed through the module. Students should not hesitate to contact them by email whenever help is needed. The tutors themselves were students in the past; hence they can identify with students' needs and anxieties, and will always be supportive.

9.   SUMMARY

Section One of this introductory book has almost been completed. But before concluding this section, it is worth summarising the main areas which have been included.

EXERCISE 14:

a) Before reading the summary provided below, summarise this section. Write approximately 20 lines. Do not look back through the pages as you write your summary.

9.1   AN OVERVIEW

Section One provided an introduction to distance learning and presented an outline of the central components of the distance learning approach to contemporary education. Students studying this section will also have been familiarising themselves with several of the techniques and strategies of the distance learning approach. These techniques can be used effectively as students proceed to Sections Two and Three of this book, and after this to a first complete module.

- The section commenced with an extended reflection on lifelong education and distance learning. Students were reminded that, to some extent at least, all adults engage in lifelong learning. Lifelong learning is so much a part of everyday living that it frequently occurs without people pausing to think about what has been learned, or even to realise that new learning experiences are happening all the time.

- Some instances of lifelong learning are more formalised, for example, adult education and, in particular, this distance learning approach to theology. Students have been introduced to the phenomenon of distance learning and, as some of its characteristics were described, students have been gently warned to be ready to deal with the loneliness of the long-distance learner.

- Engaging in distance learning requires a new way of thinking about education, a way that is quite different from the traditional way. There are many benefits to the distance learning approach; some of these were discussed specifically in relation to theology and to adult faith development.

- The section then progressed to a reflection about learning as an adult. This involved a brief analysis of the components of learning, followed by an emphasis on the distinctive characteristics of adult learning. Among the most significant of these characteristics mentioned was the mature students' existing framework of ideas which provide an appropriate context for the new concepts being learnt. Also, it was noted that there is generally more freedom and flexibility associated with adult learning.

- A brief outline was given of the structure of each module in terms of its units, sections and parts.

- During this section, interaction with the written text and other material was stressed. In order that the learning process might occur satisfactorily, students were encouraged to do the numerous exercises designed to facilitate interaction.

- Finally, students were invited to think about the central role that reading plays in the successful completion of any distance learning module. The importance of writing regularly, and of taking various kinds of notes, was emphasised. Serious attention to accuracy and detail is essential when taking notes. Some useful comments and helpful advice regarding assignments and academic tutors were included.

EXERCISE 15:

a) Return for a few moments to Exercise 1. Read your answers to the questions. Having completed this section, have your hopes, expectations and fears changed as you have progressed? If they have changed, note the changes.

b) Read the objectives for this section which were outlined in paragraph 1.1 (p.5). Do you think they have been satisfied? Write a few comments about how they have/have not been satisfied. You will have the opportunity to discuss your comments with lecturers and other students on one of the study days.

10. CONCLUSION

Congratulations! You have completed the first section of distance learning and, in doing so, have achieved the first of your targets – completing the first section of this book.

Hopefully this comprehensive overview of adult education, and the distance learning approach in particular, is sufficient to encourage students to enter more fully into the study of theology. Before proceeding to Section Two, students should take a short break, after which they should continue their studies with enthusiasm and confidence because students now know that, with adequate commitment and effort, the work will progress with satisfaction and success. Enjoy the remainder of the book.

SECTION TWO:
INTRODUCING THEOLOGY

1. WELCOME

1.1 WHO, WHAT AND WHERE?

Section Two of this book introduces students to the study of theology. Having become familiarised with some of the principles and techniques of distance learning, students will now be asked to put those principles and techniques into practice.

Because this is an introductory book, one to be followed by more comprehensive modules dealing with specific areas of Christian theology, the theological reflections of students at this time will of necessity be limited. But to begin, the following questions will be asked concerning theology itself:

- What is theology?
- Who does theology?
- In what context is theology done?

In answering these questions, students will use several theological concepts about which they already have some knowledge, and other concepts about which they will have only a vague notion. Most of these terms and concepts will be expanded in later modules.

After completing this section students should have a basic understanding of what theology is about and how theological thinking is at work in everyday life. If students discover terms that are not understood, then the glossary in Appendix Five should be consulted. Appendix Three, which provides biographical notes on many of the theologians and other thinkers to which reference is made throughout this book, may also be consulted.

Theology and biblical studies, as already stated in the introduction, are fascinating subjects to study. Even though each student's reasons for enrolling for a particular module may be different from other students' reasons, all will probably share an interest in exploring the Christian faith and have a desire to reflect on how God impinges on life and the life of the world around us. Hopefully, students will enjoy their reading and reflection and, in addition, will acquire new knowledge.

1.2 OBJECTIVES OF THIS SECTION

Once students have completed this section, they should be able to:

a)   define theology; and

b)   identify at least five theological questions of contemporary significance.

If students are unsure about what 'objectives' means in this context, consult the introduction to Section One. After students have completed this section and Section Three, they will be asked to return again to those objectives in order to discover whether or not they have been achieved.

theos
logos

2.   THEOLOGY AND THEOLOGIANS

2.1   WHAT IS THEOLOGY?

It is always an informative exercise to trace the source and formation of words (their etymology). The English word 'theology' is derived from the two Greek words *theos*, meaning God, and *logos*, meaning knowledge or study. So theology, literally, means the knowledge of God, or discourse about God.

Christian theology is the study of the God of Jesus Christ. It focuses on Christ's person and teaching; it is the methodical effort to understand God's revelation of Himself in Christ.

St Anselm of Canterbury (who lived in the eleventh century ce) described theology as 'faith seeking understanding' (Latin: fides quaerens intellectum) implying that, in the study of theology, it is faith that guides a person's reasoning. In other words, theology scrutinises the contents of belief using reason, enlightened by faith, to gain a deeper grasp of God's revelation.

faith seeking
understanding

EXERCISE 16:

a) *Read the chapter entitled 'Why do Theology?' from* Faith in Search of Understanding: An Introduction to Theology *(1991) by Charles Hill, an Australian theologian (See Appendix Four, pp. 45-47).*

b) *Hill begins this chapter by writing that 'we are supposed to be rational animals – if not always reasonable'. What does he mean? Write 3 lines.*

c) *Do you agree that doing theology is as natural for us believers as reasoning is for all human beings? Write 5 lines.*

d) *Write a definition of theology that you might submit for inclusion in a secondary school dictionary.*

2.2   THE OBJECT OF THEOLOGY

If ordinary people were asked for their ideas about what theology is, their responses would probably be quite varied, but would surely include the following:

- theology is the study of God;

- theology is an exploration of religious belief;

- theology is an intellectual probing of Christian doctrine; and

- theology is the questioning of contemporary issues of faith and morality.

Theology enquires not only into the nature of God in God's Self, but also into every aspect of the universe and of human existence. Hence, each of the responses listed above reflects some element of theology, but there is much, much more. Examples of specifically theological questions are:

a)   Does God exist?

b)   How can we know anything about God?

c)   Is Jesus Christ truly God and truly human?

d)   Can we save ourselves, or are we dependent on Christ for salvation?

e)   What is the relationship between Christ and the Church?

f)   If God is good, why do innocent people suffer?

SECTION TWO

g)   From where does evil come?

h)   Does sin still exist?

i)   How do we decide what is right and what is wrong?

j)   Is there life after death and what happens when we die?

k)   Is everything written in the Bible true?

l)   May we disagree with the Church?

m)   Do we have a responsibility to care for the earth?

n)   Why is prayer important?

o)   Are the sacraments still relevant to our lives?

p)   Is Christianity the only valid religion?

q)   What does it mean to be a believer?

Because this is an introductory book, only two of the above questions will be studied briefly – those concerning revelation (How can we know about God?) and faith (What does it mean to be a believer?). These will be studied in the next section. Students will have ample opportunity to study the remainder of these questions in subsequent modules.

2.3   THEOLOGY AS EXPLORATION

Life abounds with mysteries which challenge us. If they are solved, they are no longer mysteries. However, God remains the Ultimate Mystery who is forever beyond the grasp of our understanding. Thomas Aquinas (c. 1225-1274 ce) was one of the greatest theologians the Church has ever known. He loved talking about God and wrote profoundly on the Mysteries of God. Yet towards the end of his life he was reduced to silence. He told his friend and colleague Reginald of Piperro (c. 1230-1290 ce) that all his words and teaching were 'just straw' compared to what he had glimpsed in prayer. His words and ideas had come to an end, just as they always do for those who study the Mystery of God. But despite the difficulties in finding words for God's Mysteries, theologians must listen to the poets and mystics who remind us that we should not cease our exploration. There is in each of us an experience of restlessness and a reluctance to settle for less, but rather to journey on, to transcend the boundaries.

We realise that we will never, ever, come close to a full understanding of God. Ironically, to succeed in fully explaining God would be to put Him under our control. Then God would no longer be God, and we would no longer be God's creatures. We would have become God and God would be our creation.

EXERCISE 17:

a)   *Read the chapter entitled 'Belief in God' from* Exploring the Christian Faith *(1994) by Hubert J. Smith (See Appendix Four: pp. 48-53). Smith is a United Reformed Church minister in the United Kingdom. The chapter is divided into two parts:*

i.   *What is God like? and*

i.   *Does God exist?*

b)   *Spend some time thinking about the discussion points on pages 5-6 and pages 9-10 [pp. 50-51 and pp. 52-53] of this chapter. Write 3 lines in answer to each point. Do not worry if you are unsure about all the answers at this stage. Write what you think at this time. You will be able to return to these discussion points again at a later stage.*

2.4   THE CHALLENGE TO THEOLOGY

Nowadays, the very existence of theology as an academic subject is challenged by non-believers, especially by some who work in the media, in education and in the natural sciences. Such is the dominance of their secular world-view that in many institutions the study of theology has been re-classified as 'religious studies', 'comparative religion' or 'the philosophy of religion', disciplines which try to understand religion as a phenomenon, but not necessarily as the attempt to understand God, or faith in God. Theology, however, has always strenuously met this challenge, and today it has taken on a new vigour within the Christian tradition.

Throughout this programme, theology is treated as an academic discipline like any other, and is subject to the same rigorous intellectual standards that apply elsewhere.

EXERCISE 18:

a) *Consult a dictionary or encyclopaedia, or search the internet for definitions or descriptions of religious studies, comparative religion and the philosophy of religion.*

b) *Write 10 lines about their similarities and differences.*

2.5   WHO IS A THEOLOGIAN?

There is no doubt that for a long time theology was deemed to be the domain of an elite group of professionals and clerics. In an earlier era, the monasteries and universities were the places where theologians worked and taught.

Today we are witnessing a widening of interest in theology. In an age when the comfortable certainties of our inherited traditions are being questioned, we find people who are not content to leave their thinking to others but who wish to explore for themselves the great issues of life that all religions explore.

A theologian, then, is anyone who, from the perspective of faith, articulates an opinion about God. Thus every committed Christian is, in fact, a theologian, and the theologian's role within the Church is to understand – and to help others to understand – something of the Mystery of God. In a sense, then, the role of the theologian is to unmask aspects of the hiddenness of God. This is a role that ought to be exercised by all believers although, obviously, those who are professionally trained may be better able to interpret and communicate the Church's teaching. Nevertheless, all Christians give witness to their belief in God by way of the lives they lead.

A theologian, then, is anyone who, from the perspective of faith, articulates an opinion about God.

EXERCISE 20:

a) *Read the chapter entitled 'Profile of a theologian' which is the conclusion of the book What is Theology? (1988) by J.J. Mueller (See Appendix Four: pp. 54-58). Mueller is an American Jesuit priest.*

b) *Mueller writes that 'knowledge is not belief' and that 'doctrine is not faith'. What does this mean? Write 10 lines.*

c) *Having reflected on the profile you have read, write your own profile as a theologian. How do you perceive yourself as a theologian at this time? Write 10 lines.*

J. J. Mueller

d) Can you think of other questions that encourage us to think theologically? List them.

e) What has prompted you to take up the study of theology? Can you find any elements in your social or personal environment out of which your theology may grow? In what ways do you understand theology being a force for a better future in your particular world? Write 5 lines.

2.6   THE CONTEXT AND METHOD OF THEOLOGY

The question as to what methodology should be used in theology is one that has provoked much interest in theological circles in recent years, so much so, that one's 'theological method' is seen as being of great relevance for one's whole study of theology. Thus it must be asked: What is theological method? And what is its place and importance in theology?

By method in theology is meant its subject, its aims, its tasks, its purpose, its presuppositions, its tools, its *modus operandi*, its range and its limitations. As Canadian theologian Bernard Lonergan (1904-1984 ce) declared,

> method is not a set of rules to be followed meticulously by a dolt. It is a framework for collaborative creativity.
>
> (Lonergan, Bernard: *Method in Theology*, 1972, London, Darton, Longman and Todd, p. xi.)

One of the most rewarding purposes to which a good theological method can be put is in reflecting on how one has arrived at the answers to one's questions. Students can uncover their methodology by reflecting on the process of their own reflecting.

The key to understanding the question of methodology is to know the context, or the problems, out of which a particular theology develops. For example, the context of social deprivation in Latin America gave rise to 'liberation theology', and gender imbalance has fostered 'feminist theology'. The more traditional theologies often began with the question of personal sinfulness. But whatever way we do theology, it must spring from a lived social or personal environment and must be constantly in dialogue with that environment.

Those who have experienced only powerlessness, those who have been rendered 'invisible' by their gender or by their social or political milieu, are finding in theology a powerful and compelling way of breaking out of their confines. Thus women and indigenous peoples, racially oppressed groups and impoverished slum dwellers – to list but a few – are developing their own theologies which articulate their pain and find words for their hope. This can only bode well for the future. Christians everywhere are shedding their passivity and seeking to discover a suitable language – a Christian language – to describe and discuss contemporary issues.

2.7   THE LANGUAGE OF THEOLOGY

Because the central 'object' of theology is God – one who is ultimate and inaccessible Mystery – normal language alone is quite inadequate to express theology's various insights. Students beginning theology for the first time will be struck by the manner in which theology frequently moves into metaphor, allegory, story and narrative. Some would even say that the most appropriate language for theology is poetry. How else can one address the Mystery of God? Poetry communicates by allusion and imagery – 'echoes and whispers' – more than by definition. The poet is akin to the mystic in the realisation that 'deep-down things' are simply inaccessible to plain language. And while theology should never be irrational, its expression must bear witness to the apparent ambiguity we find in our knowledge of God.

EXERCISE 21:

a) Recall a poem that you know and like. Try to express in normal prose the sentiment of the poem and realise the difficulty this poses.

b) Read the following poem, written by Gerard Manley Hopkins (1844-1889 ce):

God's Grandeur

The world is charged with the grandeur of God.
*   It will flame out, like shining from shook foil;*
*   It gathers to a greatness, like the ooze of oil*
Crushed. Why do men then now not reck his rod?

God's Created World in all it's Beauty

Person fails to heed God's (Reck) Authority (Rod)

Generations have trod, have trod, have trod;
*   And all is seared with trade; Bleared, smeared with toil;*
*   And wears man's smudge and shares man's smell: the soil*
Is bare now, nor can foot feel, being shod.

Having Lost ALL Living Beauty.

And for all this, nature is never spent;
*   There lives the dearest freshness deep down things;*
And though the last lights off the black West went
*   Oh, morning, at the brown brink eastward, springs –*
Because the Holy Ghost over the bent
*   World broods with warm breast and with ah! bright wings.*

c) Tease out some of the imagery and allusions this poem contains. Try expressing in four sentences the theological vision of the poet.

2.8   THEOLOGY AND DOCTRINE

Doctrines (or teachings) are formulated from theological reflection. They are our 'rules of faith' and they contain teachings which are normative for the Christian Church. Christian doctrines summarise and arrange the central truths about God and Jesus Christ which have been handed down to us through the apostles and developed by theologians ever since. Doctrines are important and relevant. Without doctrines, there would be no shared reference point for faith.

Doctrines are important and relevant. Without doctrines, there would be no shared reference point for faith.

EXERCISE 22:

a) List, in order of priority, what you consider to be the most important doctrines of the Christian faith.

b) Consult the Catechism of the Catholic Church to discover which doctrines the Church teaches are essential to Catholic faith.

c) Compare your lists.

d) List all the new terms to which you have been introduced in this section. If necessary, consult the glossary for explanations.

SECTION TWO

2.9   THEOLOGY AND ACTION

There is a difference between 'right living' (orthopraxis) and 'right believing' (orthodoxy) even though the two are intertwined. The deed, rather than the theory, is what defines the person, so the test of any theology is whether or not it results in right living.

The word 'praxis' means 'reflection inspired by action'. 'Praxis' must not be confused with 'practice' or 'being practical'. Praxis combines practice with theory. Both are essential. If, however, one has a flawed understanding of one's belief, then it is likely that one's practice will not be correct either.

The placement of such an emphasis on authentic living is not a modern phenomenon. It can be found in the social teaching of the Old Testament prophets and in the teachings of Christ.

EXERCISE 23:

a) Read the following New Testament passages:

i.   Luke 10:25-27. Jesus commends the 'orthopraxis' of the Samaritan and not the 'orthodoxy' of the Levite or priest. This is not to claim that Jesus condemns the orthodoxy of the priest, it only means that the priest should be practising what he teaches.

ii. James 2:14-26 and 1 John 3:16-20. In these passages James and John are not contrasting faith and good works, but contrasting living faith and dead faith.

b) Read the chapter entitled 'Theology: A Critical Reflection' from A Theology of Liberation: History, Politics, and Salvation (revised edition, 1988) by Gustavo Gutiérrez (See Appendix Four: pp. 62-67). Gutiérrez is a Peruvian Dominican priest who is described as the 'father' of liberation theology. As you read the chapter, notice Gutiérrez' emphasis on the Christian community's role in the theological task.

c) What does Gutiérrez mean when he writes that theology is 'a critical reflection on Christian praxis'? How does this function of theology differ from the other functions of theology? Write 10 lines.

3.   THEOLOGICAL TOPICS

3.1   THE CLASSIFICATION OF THEOLOGICAL TOPICS

Theology explores God and God's involvement in the universe and human history. It therefore includes several specialised disciplines, each having a distinctive function. These disciplines are classified into various categories as follows:

a)   the study of the Bible;

b)   biblical theology;

c)   historical theology;

d)   systematic theology; and

e)   practical theology.

There are alternative classifications of theology, but this one illustrates satisfactorily the main areas of study in theology.

3.2   THE STUDY OF THE BIBLE

Every Christian theologian must have a knowledge and understanding of the Old and New Testaments, of the types of literature contained in these, and of the most appropriate methods for interpreting both the Bible as a whole and each individual book within it.

3.3   BIBLICAL THEOLOGY

Biblical theology is the interpretation and explanation of the Bible's *theological* meaning. It studies individual biblical themes in the context of the Bible as a whole and provides much of the basis for the Church's preaching, prayer, spirituality and practice. It also provides resources for the formation of the Church's doctrine.

3.4   HISTORICAL THEOLOGY

Historical theology is the study of how Christianity has understood the Bible and the faith in different periods throughout Christianity. In other words, it studies the history of the development of Christian doctrine and practice from apostolic times to the present. It involves reading and interpreting the writings of the early Church teachers to discover what meaning the Christian faith had for believers in former times. Those times provide the historical and theological contexts from which each subsequent period of Christian history is studied.

3.5   SYSTEMATIC THEOLOGY

Systematic theology seeks to present in a methodical and systematic fashion the content of Christian faith under a variety of headings, for example,

a)   What is the nature of God?

b)   Is God One, is God Three?

c)   How is creation part of God's plan?

d)   Who is Jesus Christ?

e)   How does God reveal himself?

f)   What is the Church?

g)   What are the Sacraments?

h)   What is faith?

i)   What will happen at the end of time?

Furthermore, systematic theology attempts to relate the various Christian doctrines to one another. It also considers the presuppositions, sources and limitations of faith and theology. When it is influenced by the doctrinal criteria of a particular Christian denomination, systematic theology is often referred to as 'dogmatic theology'. But the two terms are not automatically interchangeable.

3.6   PRACTICAL THEOLOGY

Practical theology is the study of the application of Christian doctrine to Christian living. It includes moral theology – the study of morality in the context of Christian belief – and deals with, for example, conscience, the distinction between right and wrong, appropriate ethical behaviour, liturgy, and pastoral theology which reflects on the care of people in different life-situations.

EXERCISE 24:

a) List some of the areas of practical theology that are relevant to your involvement in the local church.

3.7   A THEOLOGICAL SYNTHESIS

The image of a tree may be used to illustrate the interrelatedness of the main areas of theology. Scripture and Tradition (the lived faith experience which is separate from but not independent of Scripture) may be compared to the roots, and just as the roots channel nutrients and provide firm foundations for the tree, so Scripture and Tradition provide us with a record of God's revelation which, in its turn, becomes the basis for all further theological reflection.

Similarly, just as the trunk of the tree gives the tree shape and strength, historical theology and systematic theology provide structure and certainty for the Church. Christian doctrine is rooted in Scripture and Tradition in the same way as the trunk of the tree grows from and is sustained by the roots of the tree.

Finally, practical theology corresponds to the branches and leaves of the tree. As the branches and leaves are extensions of the trunk, similarly practical theology is an extension of doctrine. It is the practical application in everyday life of the doctrines of faith.

SECTION THREE:
REVELATION AND FAITH

I.   INTRODUCTION

Now that the nature of theology has been explained, two theological themes can be examined:

*   revelation; and

*   faith.

This section will provide students with a brief explanation of each of these concepts – concepts about which students will surely have some personal knowledge already.

1.1   OBJECTIVES OF THIS SECTION

When students have completed this section, they should be able to:

a)   define revelation and faith; and

b)   understand the inextricable connection between revelation and faith for the Christian.

2.   REVELATION

2.1   AGNOSTICISM OR REVELATION

God chose to reveal Himself to us, not alone in human language and actions, but also in creation, in history and in His only Son. This revelation is recorded and transmitted in the Scriptures and in Tradition, and for more than two millennia it has provided the Church with an inspired foundation on which to base its life of prayer, its development of doctrine, the practice of its liturgy and its thinking on moral issues.

Today there are those who deny that this is possible. The agnostic would say that there is no value in talking about God at all because there is no way in which knowledge of God is possible for us. The atheist denies that God exists, and so rejects the validity of faith. The concept of revelation contradicts both the atheist and the agnostic. It implies that God has freely chosen to reveal Himself to us.

2.2   REVELATION – A DISCLOSURE OF GOD

'Revelation' literally means 'the removal of a veil' or 'the disclosure of what is hidden'. The Bible is rich in references to God's self-revelation, and the New Testament portrays Jesus as the unique and most perfect revelation of God. He is the Word, uttered from the essence of God. The sense of revelation as we use it in theology is not just the 'event' – it is the event as filtered through the experience, culture and faith of individuals and communities. Our religious tradition is built on a series of 'disclosure events' which have been – and still are – reflected upon and mediated through the prophets and the sacred writers.

Given the fact of God's self-revelation to us, we must distinguish it from other types of knowledge. It is the disclosure of a mystery, which remains a mystery, and which finds expression most adequately through metaphors, images and symbols. The First Vatican Council (1869-70 ce) taught that the divine truths …

> so far excel the created intellect that even after they have been given in revelation and accepted in faith, they still remain covered by the veil of faith and wrapped in a kind of darkness as long as, in this mortal life, *we are away from the Lord, for we walk by faith, not by sight* (2 Cor 5:6-7).
>
> (Denzinger, H., and Schonmetzer, A., (eds.): *Enchiridion Symbolorum, Definitionum et Declarationum de Rebus Fidei et Morum*, 36th edition, 1976, Freiburg, Herder, n. 3016)

EXERCISE 25:

a) Read Exodus 33:13-23. Here we sense the attempts of Moses to 'grasp' God by knowing Him and by seeing His face. Write 5 lines on some experience you have had that illustrates the final statement of God: 'You shall see my back, but my face you cannot see.'

2.3   REVELATION CONTINUES

Although we say that Jesus is the most perfect revelation of God, and that the content of biblical revelation cannot be changed, one cannot say (as once happened) that revelation closed with the final book of the Bible. Catholics believe, as was expressed in the teaching of the Second Vatican Council (1962-1965 ce), that a constant and ongoing disclosure of God is still taking place in the world today, transcending all divisions of religion and culture. The Council's *Constitution on Divine Revelation* (*Dei Verbum*) describes God as one who 'uninterruptedly converses'. We also say that the word of God can be reinterpreted afresh by every new generation.

If Christ is the unsurpassable revelation of God, we must remember that the 'Christ event' is also still unfolding. There is built into the revelation of Christ a 'not yet' quality. This is called the 'eschatological' dimension of revelation, which is proclaimed in the Eucharist when we sing: 'Christ has died, Christ is risen, Christ will come again.'

Eschatology is the study of the end of time and what lies beyond the end of time. It includes the ultimate destiny and purpose of the individual human being. The decree on revelation of the Second Vatican Council (*Dei Verbum*, n. 4) refers to the provisional nature of Christianity and hence its relatedness to the future.

2.4   REVELATION AND NON CHRISTIANS

While revelation has its source and origin in God's love, it is forever experienced within a human context and community. And while we understand revelation within the parameters of the Judaeo-Christian heritage, it must be acknowledged that revelation is accessible to all people of all cultures and religions. Such is the universal salvific will of God, expressed by Thomas Aquinas in the words: 'God's hands are not tied.'

Revelation is accessible to all people of all cultures and religions. Such is the universal salvific will of God, expressed by Thomas Aquinas in the words: 'God's hands are not tied.'

2.5   REVELATION IN HISTORY

Knowledge of God has been given to us in the events of salvation history (the stories and history in the Bible, beginning with Abraham and culminating in Jesus the Christ). God's activity is seen in these events, for example, the Crossing of the Red See (in Exodus 14) and the Incarnation where God freely disclosed Himself to us in the person of Jesus the Christ, the Word made flesh.

Salvation history describes the *dialogue* between God and God's people. It also describes the *stories and events* which occurred throughout the history of Israel and which culminated in the birth, life, death, resurrection and ascension of Jesus Christ, and the sending of the Holy Spirit. The Church, by its preaching of the scriptures and by its living traditions, passes on what has been revealed by God in and through Jesus Christ.

2.6   THE ROLE OF REASON

Human beings are rational creatures. We have the ability to think, and so we constantly ask questions. We use reason to make sense of God's revelation. But revelation is not the same as other forms of knowledge. Revelation cannot be described as the product of rational inquiry, because revelation is *given* to us by God, and God is beyond our finite minds. Thus reason, while essential in *dealing with revelation*, cannot provide us with all the answers. It must be combined with what God has freely revealed to us.

EXERCISE 26:

a) *Read the chapter entitled 'Reason and Revelation' from* Introduction to Theology *(revised edition, 1983) by Marianne H. Micks (See Appendix Four: pp. 68-74). Micks is an American theologian.*

b) *What role does authority play in our reasoning process? Write 5 lines.*

c) *What are the four ways in which contemporary Christians think about reason and revelation? Write a sentence about each of the four ways.*

d) *How does faith relate to reason? What is your present understanding of the relationship between faith and reason? Write 5 lines.*

3. FAITH

3.1 OUR RESPONSE TO GOD

'Faith' is the human response to the self-revelation of God. It is far more than a mental or intellectual assent; it is a trusting of one's self to the Self of God, and it colours every aspect of a Christian's life. Our great questions of meaning and purpose are all touched by our faith, by this deep sense of God who loves us and has revealed Himself to us. Linked very closely with this response of faith is the restlessness which characterises the human spirit. St Augustine, in his *Confessions*, spoke to God: 'Our hearts are restless until they rest in Thee'[2].

While faith is a response of trust between the human person and God, it is also an assent to truths which God has revealed. Needless to say, words and language are an integral part of the assent of faith. While God who reveals Himself is one and undivided, the human mind can only express this oneness by combining a multitude of different ways. Thus, it is through words, prayers, creeds and right living that the believer reaches out to the One whose Mystery is so inadequately expressed in human language.

3.2 FAITH AND REASON

The Christian tradition has always taught that faith and reason work together. Reason can prepare the way for faith and confirm it. But it cannot provide proof or evidence for faith. Faith respects evidence, but it cannot be based on it and still be faith. It is the nature of faith that it moves beyond the evidence and trusts in the hidden, intangible presence of God. This does not make faith irrational or arbitrary; it is eminently reasonable to recognise that there is a realm beyond reason's grasp. And it should be said that the very 'hiddenness' of God means that strong faith can co-exist within a mind that is also restless and questioning.

It has often been argued that, for those who believe in God, no proof is necessary, and that for those who do not believe in God, no proof is ever convincing.

Belief in God is not like other types of belief because God's existence cannot be scientifically proven. We need to remember, however, that the scientific approach to reality is only one of several possible approaches. It has often been argued that, for those who believe in God, no proof is necessary, and that for those who do not believe in God, no proof is ever convincing.

Faith, then, is both a gift from God and a human response to God.

3.3 FAITH AND SALVATION

While it is true that faith is necessary for salvation, we must be careful to note that this does not mean explicit faith in the articles of the Creed. The grace of God makes it possible for all people of good faith – even if they appear to reject Christ and the Church – to be saved. However there must be some fundamental 'reaching out' to the One who is the source and goal of all creation.

2.   Augustine: *Confessions* Book I,1.

Faith in God is a free, reasonable and personal response to God's self-revelation. God initiates this self-revelation and invites us to respond through faith which leads to knowledge and commitment, and to a share in the salvation being offered to us in Christ.

3.4   WHY BELIEVE?

It is worth asking the question 'Why believe?' This is particularly relevant for an age in which so many people claim to have no religious belief. Some of them are atheists; many are agnostics. However, life's experiences invite us to recognise a reality beyond human reality. In other words, there are dimensions to reality that transcend human experience.

Also, there are two pivotal questions that all human beings need to address at some point during their lives. The first question is: 'Who am I?' The second question is: 'How do I understand the world?' There are many different answers to these questions. However, the answer to the second question depends very much on the answer to the first question. Believing Christians, in response to God's revelation, answer the first question by acknowledging that they are made in the image and likeness of God, and that they have been saved from the consequences of sin by the death and resurrection of Jesus Christ.

EXERCISE 27:

a) *Can you think of any other pivotal questions that human beings need to address? List them.*

Our understanding of our identity as God's creatures will significantly influence our decisions about how we live in the world and how we live with one another. This, then, is why religious belief makes such a difference, especially in troubled times when belief is often rejected. In the words of Friedrich Nietzsche (1844-1900 ce) 'those who have a *why* to live, can bear with almost any *how*'.

3.5   HOW DO WE DEFINE FAITH?

Faith can be described in various ways. It is essentially a gift from God by which we freely accept God's revelation in Christ. It is a gift that we are free to accept or reject – God does not impose the gift of faith on anyone. Not surprisingly, then, faith deals with questions of the ultimate meaning of life – questions about origins, purpose and destiny. Faith teaches us that our eternal destiny is with God, and so we spend our lives seeking to do God's will.

Faith is essentially a gift from God by which we freely accept God's revelation in Christ

3.6   FAITH AND THE SCRIPTURES

When we read the Bible (both the Hebrew Scriptures and the New Testament) we quickly discover that faith, as an expression of the relationship between God and His people, becomes a 'way of life' for those who have accepted God's revelation. Faith is a living, dynamic reality. Like all genuine relationships, it is continually changing and developing. It is never static. In the Old Testament, the faith of the Israelite people was built upon God's faithfulness to the covenant with Israel. Later, in the New Testament, faith is portrayed as the acceptance of the person and saving message of Jesus Christ. It is also the acceptance of the apostles' preaching, the signs of which are repentance and conversion to a way of life that is rooted in Jesus Christ.

EXERCISE 28:

a) *Read the article supplied entitled 'Faith'. This extract is from Chapter One of* What is Theology? *by J. J. Mueller (1988) (See Appendix Four: pp 75-79). Mueller is an American Jesuit.*

b) *The Hebrew word 'emet' means to lean on something with all one's weight. How does this description help you to explain your faith? Write 5 lines.*

c) *What is the connection between faith and truth? Write 1 sentence.*

d) *Mueller devotes much attention to the concept of covenant. What is meant by the term 'covenant' and why is it so important for understanding our faith? Write 10 lines.*

e) *Summarise the main manifestations of God's covenant with the Chosen People. Write 10 lines*

f) *What do you think is the relationship between faith, hope and love? Write 3 lines.*

g) *On p. 39 [p.78], Mueller refers to A. N. Whitehead's description of God as a 'fellow sufferer who cares'. What does this mean to you? Write 5 lines.*

3.7   FAITH DEVELOPMENT

Apart from the *content* of religious faith, which has been our focus so far, attention must also be given to the *development* of faith. There are several stages through which peoples' faith may develop, ranging from the very primitive (or nursed) faith which occurs during the early years of life, to the selfless faith occurring usually only in later life. There are, of course, other stages of varying maturity in between, and it is often useful to explore the particular stage of faith that is active in our lives, so that we can better explain our attitudes and level of understanding.

EXERCISE 29:

a) *At what stage is your faith at present? Write 2 sentences.*

In conclusion, faith is a gift from God that invites us to enter into a relationship with Him. It is an assured, obedient knowledge of God's reality, power and love. It is the assurance of things hoped for, and the conviction of things not seen (see Heb 11:1).

4.   SUMMARY AND CONCLUSION

This concludes Section Three of this introductory book, Section Two having presented an overview of theology. By this stage, students have been introduced to some important terms, along with several fundamental theological concepts. In this section, the concepts of revelation and faith have been studied in greater detail. As this book has now been completed, students should have a basic understanding of what theology is about, and an understanding of theological thinking in everyday life.

EXERCISE 30:

a) Before finishing, write your own summary of Sections Two and Three. Use approximately 20 lines. Do not look back through the pages as you write your summary; instead, let this exercise be a test of your ability to recall the main points of what you have studied. This is also a test of your appreciation of the method of distance learning.

b) Return for a few moments to Exercise 1 and Exercise 15 in Section One. Read your answers to the questions.

c) Having completed this section, have your hopes, expectations and fears changed as you have progressed? If they have changed, note the changes.

d) Read the objectives for this section in 1.1 (p.33) above.

e) Do you think that they have been satisfied?

f) Write a few comments about how they have or have not been satisfied.

The entire book – A Distance Learning Approach to Theology – has now been completed. Students are now ready to begin studying their first complete module with confidence. But before moving on, students should take a well-earned rest.

SECTION THREE

APPENDIX ONE:
BIBLIOGRAPHY

Avis, Paul: *The Methods of Modern Theology – the Dream of Reason*, 1986, Basingstoke, Marshall Pickering.

Bowden, John: *Who's Who in Theology?* 1990, London, SCM Press.

Catechism of the Catholic Church, 1994, Dublin, Veritas Publications.

Evans, Terry: *Understanding Learners in Open and Distance Education*, 1994, London, Kogan Page.

Fowler, James W.: *Stages of Faith – The Psychology of Human Development and the Quest for Human Meaning*, 1981, San Francisco, Harper & Row.

Gutiérrez, Gustavo: *A Theology of Liberation – History, Politics, and Salvation*, revised edition, 1988, translated by Inda, Caridad, and Eagleton, John, London, SCM Press.

Haight, Roger: *Dynamics of Theology*, 1990, New York, Paulist Press.

Hellwig, Monika K.: *The Role of the Theologian*, 1987, Kansas, Sheed and Ward.

Hill, Charles: *Faith in Search of Understanding – An Introduction to Theology*, 1991, Dublin, Gill and Macmillan.

Hodgson, Barbara: *Key Terms and Issues in Open and Distance Learning*, 1993, London, Kogan Page.

Kaye, A.: 'Computer-Mediated Communication in Distance Education', in, Mason, R. and Kaye, R. (eds.), *Mindweave: Communication, Computers and Distance Education*, 1989, Oxford, Pergamon.

Lockwood, Fred (ed.): *Open and Distance Learning Today*, 1995, London, Routledge.

Lonergan, Bernard: *Method in Theology*, 1972, London, Darton, Longman and Todd.

Mackey, James P.: *Modern Theology – A Sense of Direction*, 1987, Oxford, Oxford University Press.

Micks, Marianne H.: *Introduction to Theology*, revised edition, 1993, New York, Seabury Press.

Mueller, J. J.: *What is Theology?* 1988, Wilmington, Delaware, Michael Glazier, Inc.

Olszewski, Daryl: *Everyday Theology for Catholic Adults*, 1991, Dublin, The Columba Press.

Parratt, John: *A Guide to Doing Theology*, 1996, London, SPCK.

Smith, Hubert J.: *Exploring the Christian Faith*, 1994, Norwich, The Canterbury Press.

Stone, Howard W., and Duke, James O.: *How to Think Theologically*, 1996, Minneapolis, Fortress Press.

Wiles, Maurice: *What is Theology?* 1976, Oxford, Oxford University Press.

APPENDIX TWO:
VERSIONS OF THE BIBLE IN ENGLISH

Authorised (King James) Version [AV; KJV]

The Authorised (King James) version is the classic Protestant translation. However, it contains language and word use that is now considered outdated and unclear. Like the Douay Rheims Bible it is often difficult to understand.

New King James Version [NKJV]

The New King James Version attempts to retain the poetry of the Authorised Version in a modern translation.

Douay Rhimes Bible

Until the Second Vatican Council (1962-1965 ce) this was the only Bible in English officially recognised by the Catholic Church as being suitable for Catholics. It is quite difficult to read because it is not a modern translation.

Jerusalem Bible

The Jerusalem Bible is an accurate and attractively poetic version of the French translation made by Dominican scholars at the École Biblique in Jerusalem. It is the version that is stipulated to be used in Catholic churches in Ireland.

The New Jerusalem Bible

The New Jerusalem Bible is a revised and updated version of the Jerusalem Bible using the results of modern research. It is widely used in Roman Catholic churches and schools.

New English Bible [NEB]

The New English Bible was the first modern translation produced by a joint committee representing the Protestant Churches of Britain and Ireland.

Revised English Bible [REB]

The Revised English Bible is a revision of the New English Bible with updated and inclusive language.

Good News Bible

The Good News Bible is an easily read ecumenical translation with inclusive language.

New International Version [NIV]

The New International Version is an accurate translation that is widely used by Protestant Churches.

Revised Standard Version [RSV]

The Revised Standard Version uses simple words and is designed for use in private and public worship. It is also suitable for study purposes because it is very faithful to the original biblical languages.

New Revised Standard Version [NRSV]

The New Revised Standard Version is an ecumenical, inclusive language edition based on the Revised Standard Version, but having the benefit of the latest scholarship. This version is extremely accurate. It is the version used by the Revised Common Lectionary (RCL) in the Church of Ireland.

New American Bible [NAB]

The Catholic Bible Society in America produced The New American Bible in order to provide a modern Catholic translation. It is the first American Roman Catholic edition to have been based on the original languages rather than on the Latin Vulgate.

Christian Community Bible [CCB]

The Christian Community Bible is produced in the Philippines as a Bible for popular use. It contains excellent notes and commentaries.

APPENDIX THREE:
BIOGRAPHICAL NOTES

ABELARD, Peter (1079-1142 ce): French philosopher and theologian.

ALBERT THE GREAT (1193-1280 ce): German Dominican theologian and scientist.

ANSELM OF CANTERBURY (1033-1109 ce): English philosopher and theologian.

ARISTOTLE (384-322 bce): Greek philosopher.

AUGUSTINE OF HIPPO (354-430 ce): Christian theologian and Bishop.

AVERROES (1126-1198 ce): Moslem lawyer and philosopher.

BARTH, Karl (1886-1968 ce): Swiss Reformed theologian.

BERNARD OF CLAIRVAUX (1090-1153 ce): Cistercian abbot.

BLONDEL, Maurice (1861-1941 ce): French Catholic lay philosopher.

BULTMANN, Rudolf (1884-1976 ce): German New Testament scholar.

BURGHARDT, Walter (1914-): American Catholic priest and theologian.

CONGAR, Yves (1904-): French Dominican theologian.

CULLMANN, Oscar (1902-): French New Testament scholar. A Lutheran layman.

GILSON, Etienne (1884-1978 ce): French philosopher and Church historian.

HEGEL, Georg (1770-1831 ce): German philosopher.

GAUNILO: Eleventh century ce French Benedictine monk.

LUTHER, Martin (1483-1546 ce): German Protestant Reformer.

LONERGAN, Bernard (1904-1985 ce): Canadian Jesuit theologian.

MARX, Karl (1818-1883 ce): German economist and philosopher.

MOLTMANN, Jürgen (1926-): German theologian of the Reformed Church.

NIETZSCHE, FRIEDRICH (1844-1900 ce): German philosopher.

PLATO (427-347 bce): Greek philosopher.

RAHNER, Karl (1904-1984 ce): German Jesuit theologian.

RUSSELL, Bertrand (1872-1970 ce): British analytic philosopher.

RICCI, Matteo (1552-1610 ce): Italian Jesuit.

SARTRE, Jean-Paul (1905-1980 ce): French existentialist philosopher.

SCHILLEBEECKX, Edward (1914-): Flemish Dominican theologian.

THOMAS AQUINAS (1225-1274 ce): Dominican theologian.

WHITEHEAD, Alfred North (1861-1947 ce): English philosopher and mathematician.

APPENDIX FOUR:
EXTERNAL READING

1

Why

'do theology'?

If I sin, what do I do to thee,
    thou watcher of men?
Why hast thou made me thy mark?
Why have I become a burden to thee?

Job 7.20

Who has inflicted this upon us? Who has made us Jews different
to all other people? Who has allowed us to suffer so terribly up
till now? It is God who has made us as we are, but it will be
    God, too, who will raise us up again.

The Diary of Anne Frank

We are supposed to be rational animals — if not always reasonable. So, puzzling things out is as normal for us as a dog worrying a bone. Things have to make sense; we must have (at least in our more reflective moments) an explanation for apparent contradictions, a reason for what happens, a basis for decision. 'To be, or not to be', ponders a worried Hamlet; 'that is the question: whether 'tis nobler in the mind to suffer the slings and arrows of outrageous fortune, or to take up arms against a sea of troubles and by opposing end them'. And people have spent a lot of time since Shakespeare trying to make sense of Hamlet too.

So theology comes naturally to us — theology as an attempt to make sense of what we believe. Hamlet, of course, was not theologising about the options open to him — only using his reason, or perhaps rationalising a soft option.

1

Charles Hill,

Faith in Search of Understanding : an introduction to theology,

Dublin : Gill and Macmillan, 1991, pp. 1-4.

Theology, St Anselm told us in the eleventh century, is 'faith seeking understanding'; our reasoning is done in the light of faith. Poor Job in Old Testament times put to himself and his friends the age-old question 'Why me?', and tried to solve it in the light of what his faith told him of God and humanity; it was not enough, and so the problem lay unanswered until God's Son in a similar predicament offered us the complete answer. At least Job was *theologising*, whereas the advice of Aristotle a little later, 'Those who wish to succeed must ask the right preliminary questions', is only a *philosopher's* wisdom or experience. No faith needed to ask questions — that's only being rational; it's when we subject our beliefs to questioning that we are theologising.

Hamlet, if philosopher rather than theologian, nevertheless highlights the fact that we can often do with prompting to bring our brains to bear on our beliefs. Trouble, suffering, persecution, the world's ills — such things start us thinking, trying to reconcile what we experience with what we believe. Which is why a lot of theology has to do with suffering and evil. Job in his generation and Anne Frank in hers, the Babylonian captivity then and the Holocaust and Hiroshima now: how do we reconcile it all with a loving God? Many cannot, and abandon reason or God in the process. 'Doing theology' is not as simple as solving an equation; Job's friends certainly had their equation wrong.

But the object of theology is not just the dark side of life; it is all of life, all that God has shared with us, and himself too — whatever our faith bears on. For Malcolm Muggeridge, the life and work of Mother Teresa of Calcutta was 'something beautiful for God'. It not only made an impression on him, it brought him to belief. 'For me, Mother Teresa of Calcutta embodies Christian love in action. Her face shines with the love of Christ on which her whole life is centred, and her words carry that message to a world that never needed it so much'.

My own impression of Mother Teresa, for what it is worth, was of someone who is conspicuously short on theologising, almost fundamentalist in her acceptance of a gospel others of us worry over. I heard her say this: 'I remember one day they brought a man half of whose body was eaten up with cancer. He was so smelly that nobody could stand with him. I happened to be in the house with him and I started washing him. And he said to me, "Why are you doing this?" And I said to him what Jesus said. He was a Hindu man and I told

him what Jesus had said. And I said, "I really believe I am touching his body in you". And then he said, "Glory to Jesus Christ through you!" And I said, "No, but glory to Jesus Christ through you, because you are sharing in his passion".' Such literalism comes as a shock to a professional theologian, suggesting the limits of mere theology.

A reminder here that theology is not all books and words. People have expressed their faith and the questions it raises for them in other forms. Whereas conventional painters have represented the Christian mysteries in a soothing manner, to study a Dali or Chagall or El Greco is to set us wondering what meaning the artist found in the biblical text. The comfortable crucifixions of Old Masters contrast starkly with the tortured Cristo of a Third World artist painting out of a situation of oppression and deprivation that has made him read the Gospels differently. The melodrama of a medieval *Stabat Mater* or *Dies Irae* suggests an interpretation of the scriptural text that biblical scholars today would deny was the purpose of the evangelists, who were more interested in austere dogmatic truth than in heart-rending pathos. All these creative artists have in their own way, rightly or wrongly, theologised about their beliefs before putting paint to canvas or music to notation.

So 'doing theology' is natural for us believers, as reasoning is for all human beings. Perhaps like Hamlet we can think too much, and like Mother Teresa we should instead move directly from faith to action. But there will be times — dark times as well as luminous ones — when our faith will seek understanding, and the habit that theology is will stand us in good stead. It is a habit to be developed; the following pages suggest how this can be done and in fact has been done by believers down the ages.

The world needs theologians. Yes, this absurd little earth, where a billion humans fall asleep hungry, this glorious globe that was freed from slavery by the crucifixion of its God, this paradoxical planet that nurtures love and hate, despair and hope, skepticism and faith, tears and smiles, wine and blood, this creation of divine love where men and women die for one another and kill one another — this world desperately needs theologians.

Why? To interpret this bittersweet experience, this bloody mess, to ask what it's all about. And precisely this is the theologian's task: struggling, agonizing to understand and express. It is your privilege and your burden to search out *where* God has spoken, where God speaks: from the burning bush in

2

3

Charles Hill,

<u>Faith in Search of Understanding : an introduction to theology,</u>

Dublin : Gill and Macmillan, 1991, pp. 1-4.

1

Why 'do theology'?

Midian to the gas ovens in Auschwitz, from the word that was creation to the Word that was made flesh, from the church gathered in council to the skin-and-bones dying that defecate at Calcutta's curbstones, from the Book that somehow reveals the heart of God to the trace of God on the face of humanity.

W. Burghardt, 'This world desperately needs theologians', *Catholic Mind* 79 (March 1981) 34

Some relevant reading

Carmody, J. and Carmody, D., *Contemporary Catholic Theology*, Harper and Row, San Francisco, 1985.

Fisher, K. and Hart, T., *Christian Foundations. An Introduction to Faith in Our Time*, Paulist, New York, 1986.

Monk, R. and Stamey, J., *Exploring Christianity*, Prentice Hall, Englewood Cliffs, 1984.

Shelly, B., *Church History in Plain Language*, Word Books, Waco, 1982.

Exercises in theology

(1) We often find ourselves puzzling over life's injustices, pleasant surprises, and the twists and turns of fate. Do we acknowledge that this can involve theologising as we endeavour to reconcile daily events with our beliefs?

(2) We see and hear much theology — good and bad — in the Old Masters and modern composers and artists. Choose a hymn, a painting, or piece of writing that involves expression of belief, and trace the author's attempt to bring understanding to faith.

(3) At what age do children begin to ponder their faith, to make sense of what they (or the faith community) believe — in other words, to theologise? Have you thought about the place of theology in religious education? (You may care to glance ahead to Chapter 13).

THE PRIORY INSTITUTE : DISTANCE LEARNING PROGRAMME : THEOLOGY FOR TODAY : A DISTANCE LEARNING APPROACH TO THEOLOGY

Hubert J. Smith
Exploring the Christian Faith
Norwich : The Canterbury Press 1994
pp. 1 - 10.

1 | Belief in God

● *This opening topic is fundamental to all that comes afterwards, so it will not be surprising to find that it is more substantial in its content than the rest. In order to break it up into manageable parts for study purposes, it has been divided into two sections, each with its own discussion points. The first section introduces some of the different ideas of God's nature which are to be found in the Bible, and raises the question of what God is believed to be like. The second section then moves to an exploration of a more philosophical kind: how do we know that God exists at all? Are there any proofs of his existence? Study groups are advised to deal with these two sections separately, because although they are clearly related, nevertheless they are quite different in their approaches, and in any case there is far too much material here to be covered in a single session.*

(a) WHAT IS GOD LIKE?

Christians believe in God. But are all Christians agreed about what God is like? The Apostles' Creed (which, incidentally, was not actually written by the Apostles) opens with the words 'I believe in God . . .' and goes on to describe him as 'the Father Almighty, maker of heaven and earth'. But this is not really much help. The creed was almost certainly meant as a personal statement of faith, for use by people who were about to be initiated into the Church through baptism, and was never intended to be used as a thorough-going analysis of developed theology. It shows only that this is the point at which Christian faith begins. We must take the matter further.

It is sometimes supposed that the Bible provides us with a detailed and coherent picture of God's nature, but closer examination shows that this is not the case. Careful study of the Old and New Testaments reveals that there are many different concepts of God to be found there, and they are not always entirely consistent with one another. Evidently the people of Bible times had a wide variety of ideas about what God is like. We can begin by looking at some of the ways in which God is portrayed in the Bible.

Old Testament pictures of God

In some parts of the Old Testament – especially the oldest parts – God is thought of as one deity among others. People imagined that every nation had its own god, who protected them in an exclusive kind of way. The ancient Israelites commonly believed that their own god (known to them by the name of YAHWEH) was more powerful than the others, but nevertheless he was not the only deity. We can see this idea brought out very plainly in the following passage:

Judges 2:11–15

● *Here it is said that the Israelites forsook their own god and worshipped the gods of other nations – identified in this instance as the Canaanite Baalim and Ashtaroth. Nowhere in this passage do we find it suggested that these other gods were false, or that they did not exist: they are represented as real rivals to the god of the Israelites.*

This belief in local tribal gods is sometimes known as Henotheism – a word which was coined in the middle of the nineteenth century to distinguish it from Monotheism (belief that there is only one God) and Polytheism (belief that there are many deities who are all equal in power and status). Most Biblical scholars consider that the religion of Israel was Henotheistic at first, and only gradually developed into Monotheism.

We can see a similar idea of God expressed in one of the Psalms. Look at:

Psalm 137:1–6

● *This psalm was written during the period when the Hebrew people were prisoners-of-war in the empire of Babylon (sixth century BC). The author evidently believed that God could be worshipped only in the Jerusalem Temple, and that it was impossible to worship on foreign territory. Here again is a very localised idea of God, though it is not entirely clear whether the writer of this psalm believed that God himself was absent from Babylon, or whether God would not accept worship from anywhere other than the Temple.*

Compare this with the sentiments of another psalm. Look at:

Psalm 139:1–12

● *This writer has a very different understanding of God. For him, it is impossible to go anywhere without finding that God is already there. Heaven and Hell, darkness and light are all the same to God, who dwells everywhere and knows everything. This omnipresent and omniscient God is very far removed from the territorial deity of Psalm 137.*

Gradually the people of the Old Testament came to an awareness that there is only one true God, and that idols simply do not have any reality. Look at:

Isaiah 45:18 to 46:7

● *This anonymous prophet of the sixth century BC (usually referred to as Deutero-Isaiah) categorically denies that other gods exist, and mocks those who manufacture their own deities. He points out that these home-made gods are incapable of doing anything at all.*

It was only when belief in one all-powerful and universal God came into currency that it was possible to think of him as having created the whole universe, and possessing dominion over it. Such a claim would have been impossible for those who thought only in terms of local gods with restricted authority, unless they were also dimly conscious of a 'higher' God than those with merely territorial concerns.

characteristics. Again, these are extremely varied. Where God is pictured as a tribal deity it is common to find him portrayed as a warrior, who leads his people into battle and guarantees victory over their enemies. We can see an example of this:

Exodus 15:3–5

● *In this passage it is openly said that God (YAHWEH) is a warrior, and that the escape from Egypt is to be counted as one of his greatest victories. There are many such passages to be found throughout the earlier parts of the Old Testament.*

Another dominant idea is that of God as a shepherd, who protects and guides his flock, ensuring that they have sufficient for their needs. The well-known Psalm 23 brings this out extremely well. Here, the warrior image has virtually disappeared, and in its place there is found a gentler conception of a devoted and loving deity. It was this image which dominated much of what Jesus had to say, both about God and about himself.

But by far the most telling imagery used about God is that of a parent – usually a father-figure, but not necessarily always in gender terminology. Indeed, in the book of Hosea (11:1–4) there is a very touching passage suggestive of maternal tenderness which contrasts very starkly with the warrior-like picture described above. God is thought of as having fatherlike characteristics: he gives life, he feeds his 'children', he teaches them, he controls and disciplines them, he protects them, and most of all he loves them. We have become so accustomed to the Biblical idea of God as a father-figure that it comes as something of a surprise to discover that in the religion of Islam this sort of imagery is considered highly improper. Muslims never refer to God as 'Father', on the ground that it suggests an over-intimate relationship with the holy deity.

New Testament pictures of God

In the New Testament the emphasis of all the writers is largely upon the way in which Jesus reveals God's nature and purposes to humankind. Jesus is the one who shows what God is like, and in that sense there is a much sharper focussing of thought. Supremely, Jesus shows a loving God who is prepared to sacrifice even himself because of his great love for his people. Sometimes the Old Testament ideas are recalled, as in the following passage:

Romans 1:19–25

● *In this passage St Paul gives the classical Old Testament picture of God as possessing everlasting power, and who cannot be represented by manufactured idols. Paul adds that God's nature can also be perceived within the created order (i.e. the universe) – another Old Testament idea, to be found for example in Psalm 19:1, except that here Paul gives it a moral content.*

The moral teachings of the New Testament also clearly echo the Old Testament ideas of a God who is himself just and fair, and who expects the same from his people. But it is the concept of God as 'Father' which tends to dominate, and in particular it is the relationship of Jesus to God which lies at the heart of New Testament thought. Jesus is God's obedient son, who lives in such close communion with his Father that he is 'one' with him. Thus, according to the author of the Fourth Gospel, whoever has seen Jesus has effectively seen God. As we have set aside a later topic about Jesus it is not necessary to develop this point here, except to lay stress upon the way in which the New Testament writers hold up Jesus as the revelation both of God and also of redeemed humanity.

DISCUSSION POINTS

1. **Is there a right or wrong way of thinking about God's nature? If so, how do we know which is which?**
2. **How can Jesus the man reveal the nature of the eternal God?**

3. **If the writers of the Bible held differing views about what God is like, should we conclude that it is all a matter of personal opinion?**

4. **Can a Christian subscribe to the idea of a warrior-God?**

5. **If there is only one God, what are we to make of the other religions of the world?**

6. **If God is as powerful as the Bible claims, why does he allow so much to go wrong in his universe?**

7. **Is it true, as some have suggested, that the God described in the Old Testament is not the God revealed by Jesus Christ?**

(b) DOES GOD EXIST?

The people who wrote the Bible took it for granted that God exists. Apart from one or two fleeting references (such as Psalm 14:1, repeated in Psalm 53:1), hardly anyone seems to have questioned the reality of God. His existence was axiomatic. But in modern times the issue is a serious one. Scientific discoveries have made people less ready to accept what cannot be proved, and today there are many who find it impossible to believe in the existence of God. Technically these people are known as ATHEISTS, and the word suggests that they have weighed the evidence and have concluded that there is no such being as God. They are to be distinguished from AGNOSTICS, who, strictly speaking, are those who admit that they do not know whether God exists or not. They are not persuaded one way or the other. In practice, however, atheists and agnostics are much the same because both are 'unbelievers'.

From time to time Christians are invited to state the grounds of their belief in God, and it is at this point that many find themselves in considerable difficulty. They sometimes respond with statements such as 'It's all a matter of faith', or perhaps 'I just believe, and that's that'. Such answers, though no doubt sincere, are hardly likely to be persuasive, and for this

reason Christian philosophers down the centuries have tried to demonstrate that there are genuine reasons why belief in God is sound. Of these philosophers, two in particular stand out as of great importance, namely, St Anselm of Canterbury and St Thomas Aquinas. Obviously there have been many others, but nearly all later arguments about God's existence are derived from these two thinkers, and we can look now at what they said.

St Anselm of Canterbury

Anselm was Archbishop of Canterbury in the eleventh century, and was actually a contemporary of William the Conqueror. He put forward what has since come to be known as the ONTOLOGICAL ARGUMENT – a somewhat grand name for a difficult piece of logical reasoning. Put in rather simplistic terms, it looks like this:

● *'God is the greatest being that it is possible to imagine. Therefore he must exist, because if he lacked existence it would be possible to imagine a greater being who does exist.'*

At first sight the argument seems silly – and it comes as no surprise to discover that even in his own time Anselm's argument was challenged. A monk by the name of Gaunilo retorted by saying that there is a big difference between claiming that God 'must' exist and saying that he actually does exist. Gaunilo pointed out that to imagine something to exist does not mean that it really is 'there'. He said that someone might imagine a very beautiful island in the middle of the ocean, and even imagine in great detail what it might look like: but this did not mean that such an island existed. To some people, Anselm's reasoning seems very much like that of those who say that because they believe in God, God must therefore be real – at least to them.

Anselm's argument, however, is not as childish as it may appear to be. It is really very subtle. He answered Gaunilo by saying that the existence of God could not be compared to the existence of an imaginary island, and that Gaunilo had failed to understand the nature of the Ontological argument. There are many philosophers today who take Anselm's reasoning very seriously.

St Thomas Aquinas

Rather more persuasive arguments were put forward in the thirteenth century by St Thomas Aquinas, whose name is especially revered in the Roman Catholic Church. He disliked Anselm's way of reasoning, largely because it depended upon hypothesis, and he himself preferred to reason on the basis of actual experience and evidence. He proposed several arguments of a fairly detailed nature, but here we can note two in particular – expressed once again in a simplified way:

● *Everything that we see around us clearly has been caused by something before it. Every event was preceded by a prior event. Therefore there must have been a 'First Cause' for everything, and this we understand to be God.*

● *Everything that we see in the world is part of a highly complicated design, with things being dependent upon other things. Everything appears to have a place and a purpose within the overall pattern. Since such a world could not have come about by accident, it is therefore necessary to believe that it is the work of a Great Designer, and this we believe to be God.*

Although these arguments were put forward many centuries ago, they are still discussed today. However, they are not universally accepted as sound. First of all, it has been pointed out that if everything really does have a prior cause, then there cannot logically be a 'first cause' because it would immediately be an exception to the rule upon which the whole argument depends. It cuts the ground from under its own feet, because the 'first cause' would need to have a prior cause too.

Second, not everyone is convinced that there is a genuine pattern or design evident in the universe. Some consider that the alleged design is no more than our human way of looking at things, and that in reality the universe is a tangled mass of elements which are competing with each other rather than providing mutual support. And of course it therefore follows that if there is no genuine design, then we cannot conclude that there is a Great Designer.

Third, many philosophers have remarked that even if it could be shown that there is a First Cause or a Great Designer, it does not necessarily follow that, as St Thomas Aquinas claimed, 'this is what we believe to be God'. Certainly neither of the arguments leads to proof of the existence of the kind of God of whom the Bible speaks – that is, a God who has a special loving relationship with human beings. The so-called 'proofs' may indeed point in the general direction of some almighty power or force, but they do not (and cannot) lead to a fully-developed Christian belief in the God revealed in the person and work of Jesus Christ.

If all this seems somewhat negative, it is currently being argued that the concept of 'proof' is the product of a scientific way of thinking, and that since science, by its very nature, can deal only with the world of verifiable 'things' it cannot be summoned to give a verdict upon matters of religious faith. If it tries to do so, it steps outside its proper sphere and thereby ceases to be genuinely scientific. Therefore the person who believes in God need not be too anxious if his or her beliefs fail the tests of scientific or logical enquiry. There are other more appropriate tests, which may not succeed in convincing the sceptical but will certainly satisfy the believer.

DISCUSSION POINTS

1. **Are there any contemporary arguments which might persuade a non-Christian that God exists? Are the arguments of Anselm and Aquinas still acceptable?**

2. If it could be proved that God exists, would there still be any need for religious faith?

3. 'God is a theory proposed by people who don't understand the world around them. One day, science will make belief in God unnecessary.' Do you agree?

4. Are there any arguments against the existence of God? If so, what are they?

5. Is there any difference between a religious belief which is reached through reasoning and one which is reached through simple faith?

6. Do the arguments for the existence of God also point towards the existence of a Devil?

J. J. Mueller,

What is Theology ?

Wilmington, Delaware
Michael Glazier, Inc., 1988, pp. 91 - 98.

Conclusion:
Profile of a Theologian

Our study began with human anthropology as the context for theology. We found that the major building blocks of theology in the origin myth of Genesis are sin, salvation, and faith (Part I). Each building block supports additional concepts such as the Kingdom of God, grace, obedience, hope, and love. Then we saw that theological anthropology finds its key relationships in the understanding of Jesus, God, and us (Part II). Theology revolves around our understanding of these three topics, taken both individually and together. Finally, we identified the sources for our understanding of these topics and relationships, which take the form of language and texts (Part III). It seems only fitting to end where we began: with the human person.

We will speak of a specific human person: you, the reader. What happens to you when you study theology? While this is impossible to determine ahead of time, we can see what happens to others. The conclusion of our study will take the form of a reflection about being a theologian. Although this description does not pretend to be complete or normative in any sense, it does purport to be a common profile. The contention is that if one enters into the study and doing of theology, then one can expect to find changes occurring in one's self. One enters into the fundamental questions of life and the most basic commitments human persons make. One enters one's own conversion process. The profile of a theologian is a metaphor of what might happen to anyone. The following reflection seeks, first or all, to stimulate, evoke, and encourage each person in his or her pursuit of theology. Secondly, it indicates that one is never alone

in doing theology—one does theology in a tradition and within a community of believers. Thirdly, each person's contribution to theology is most welcome and puts the richness of his or her faith experience at the disposal of others. As good theology, it always serves the Lord and others. Good theology is good ministry.

Profile of a Theologian

Above all, the theologian is a disciple. Luke gives us this image in his description of the life of Jesus as a journey. Beginning in Galilee to the north and stretching to Jerusalem in the south, this journey represents the personal following of the will of God. Geography is itself a metaphor for the journey every person makes in returning to the Father. Journey is the symbol of the life of a disciple. One not only learns but also follows the master wherever he goes. As the model of discipleship, Jesus obeyed the Father. Jesus leaned upon God with all his weight (the definition of faith) and he proclaimed the Kingdom of God. His faith took him to different towns, to the outcast and the marginal; in short, wherever the Spirit led. Wherever he went and to whomever he met, he showed both his love and that of the Father. Jesus showed his love in compassion, in forgiveness, in solidarity with the poor. And when people came to him, he told them to follow him. Those who did became disciples.

The profile of a theologian might best be glimpsed in Luke's culminating story of the two men on their way to Emmaus. On that Easter morning, they had left the other disciples and journeyed away from Jerusalem. Discouraged, confused, seeking answers, they talked. A stranger came up behind them and greeted them, asking what they were speaking about. They were shocked that the stranger did not know about Jesus' death in Jerusalem. And, they continued, women had just returned from the tomb saying that his body had disappeared. They had believed in Jesus but they did not understand.

As they walked, the stranger began to interpret the scriptural text about how the son of man would have to suffer and so enter into glory. Things began to make sense; the interpretation

became clearer. Unwilling to let the stranger go, they asked him to stay for dinner. While at dinner, they recognized him "in the breaking of the bread." Then he disappeared. They ran back to their friends in Jerusalem to tell them what happened and how their hearts had burned with the truth that came with understanding.

Theologians' hearts have not stopped burning since. Nor have they kept their understandings quiet. The truth seeks to reveal itself and, while no theologian claims to hold the whole truth, each theologian renders it the best way he or she can. Jesus continues to disappear just as he did for the two disciples. Theologians seek to recognize his presence wherever and whenever he appears. It is not insignificant that the two disciples found Jesus in "the breaking of the bread", a common reference to the Eucharistic liturgy. Often the theologian finds God—or rather God finds the theologian—in ordinary events and symbols. The theologian tries to understand and articulate the meaning of the relationship.

The journey requires the entire person and asks for a complete conversion: intellectual, affective, moral, and religious. Along the way, the theologian offers his or her understanding of this journey to others. As the two disciples on the way to Emmaus show us, the life and work of a theologian remain always that of a disciple on a journey.

The theologian freely chooses, as a disciple, to enter the discipline of theology. He or she then studies, learns the tradition, the methods, the content, the classics, etc., in an attempt to become competent. Because theology depends upon a community of interpretation, a basic minimum of training is usually required. Although academic degrees do not measure faith, they do provide a measure of competency. On paper, degrees indicate a type of training and professional achievement. Some degrees are ecclesiastical degrees, conferred by a particular religious tradition, e.g., S.T.D. (Doctorate in Sacred Theology). Others are academic degrees conferred by universities, e.g., Ph.D. or M.A.. Each theologian has different strength: research, interpretation, communication, pastoral, systematizing, constructive, or practical skills. No one possesses all of them, yet every one of these skills is needed.

to earn it. A degree does not tell us what challenges the person encountered, or what results he or she achieved in motivation, belief, life, and faith. The degree actually represents both a level of training achieved and a type of program undertaken. But it means little if the theologian has not begun the process of personal integration. In sum, a person is educated in theological skills and competency.

The journey, even through academic programs, is not always what one expects. In fact, one might advise the student to expect the unexpected. Challenges will come up from behind, as did the stranger at Emmaus.

I remember one example very vividly in my own program. I was doing a degree in historical theology, and the history of the popes, potentates, inquisition, crusades, schisms, and political decisions had left me in the pit of disillusionment. How could God be working this way? Is this the Church I love, where I have found God's love? It challenged me emotionally, intellectually, and religiously. I was changing. Over a period of time, almost like spring supplanting winter, my consternation and confusion began to change. I passed from an intellectual to an emotional conversion to a faith conversion. Growing inside was a deeper and wider and more pervasive trust in the Holy Spirit. If the Spirit could work through so many human obstacles, and the Church continue to preach the good news, and people continue to encounter God in the Church, then indeed the promise of the Lord's Spirit within us was evident. God did not remove our human foibles. God trusts us more than I could imagine. At the edge of losing my faith was a deeper appreciation of salvation and human cooperation. It seemed that it was necessary to lose my presuppositions, intellectual convictions, and emotional preferences in order to find a deeper and purified faith. This experience has continued to be an important parable in my life concerning the unexpected twists and turns of this journey.

While I experienced this conversion in theology, others have similar experiences at worship, in ethical questions, in human relationships. Through each experience, compassion for the human journey with God grows. God and his mysterious ways become more and more central to life: faith in God is the bottom line of every spirituality, especially the theologian's.

Instead of coming up with clear precise answers, theologians open for us a richer diversity of options and the encouragement to follow God in the discipleship to which he calls us.

In decades past, theologians were like homesteaders who had a piece of land, a farm, and fences. Life was clear, chores were constant and regular, life was calm. Theology gave answers. Today, theologians resemble pioneers. They have pulled up stakes, harnessed the wagons, and set off for new and unknown territories. Theology is moving, unsettled, searching for and discovering new territories and peoples. Theology today has more questions than answers, and its answers are less absolute. Moving viewpoints have replaced static ones; the journey has replaced the homestead as metaphor.

Theologians are disciples in the middle of a journey. Because the theologian is a person of faith, of the church, and of the world, the ups and downs of events, people, and him or herself affect the theology. The theologian knows both sides, and the tension between them. Placed as a mediator of the tradition, an interpreter of the past and present, the theologian knows the Church's good points and bad. On the one hand the theologian knows of the Kingdom of God, and on the other hand knows sexism, racism, authoritarianism, and politics in the church. On the one hand the theologian knows that love is the center of human life and on the other hand must allow people to make choices, even fail in their freedom, in order to find God. On the one hand the theologian knows of God's desire for justice, peace, and love in the world, and on the other hand sees poverty, oppression, and violence every day. Theologians do not experience something that others do not. But because of their area of study, their sensitivity is heightened. Theologians are not special; they are specialists. The way the theologian integrates these challenges will most truly reflect the basic presuppositions, direction, and tone of his or her theology.

Theologians immerse themselves in human experience. Sensitized to belief, the theologian will be tested with unbelief. Knowledge is not belief: doctrine is not faith. Begun in Adam and Eve, and continued in all humanity since, and even found in Jesus, the theologian struggles to find the will of God. In so doing, theologians enter into the depths of human unbelief, doubt, and despair. Faith requires it. The theologian cannot draw back from the journey, but must follow Jesus wherever he goes. God's promise in the resurrection is victory over sin and death. The theologian enters these areas armed only with the power of faith, hoping to emerge on the other side victorious in love. The journey is none other than the death-resurrection event of Jesus. Not all are called or chosen to enter into this redemptive action in the same way—but all are called.

Theologians are disciples for all people. Their work might come from a church tradition but it belongs to all people. We journey together as a global community. As learners, disciples help others to come in contact with what it means to be human, and with the Lord who loves us as humans. The word "education" comes from "ex" and "ducere" which mean "to lead out." The action of education is not primarily to put knowledge into a person, but to provide information and skills whereby the person can become whatever he or she wants to be. Theology is no different. Theology offers people the opportunity to develop every dimension of their selves. This requires knowledge.

For example, one's faith might begin in the family, but it grows when other people and events draw it out. One goes to school, meets others, does new activities. Faith changes in relation to these experiences. Just as a mature person does not leave the love of the family, but becomes more a part of it in different ways, so too does one not leave the faith from the family, but matures through different experiences. Knowledge works as a circle: drawing one out and returning one's self in a new way. Whether in a book, a course, a lecture, an article, or a conversation, a theologian offers people a way to see their lives.

Exposure to the word of God in Scripture often opens people to new understandings and horizons. Informing people about the meaning of Jesus, the community called Church, the sacraments, and morality provides true freedom. People's test for validity is often the "correct fit" that these explanations have with their faith experience and with what they already know to be true. A validation of truth takes place. This sounds like intuition but is not; it is knowledge of the heart as opposed to knowledge of the head. It is like two people who love one another and know the truth of that love. Through the same Holy Spirit, the Christian experience of the Lord seems to recognize itself. Hence a major part of a theologian's task is to

articulate that experience well. Instead of operating as a cut-and-dried conclusion to a syllogism, theology is persuasive. But this is not enough. We all have intellectual and emotional blockages that resist faith. A conversion process is always required, even of theologians.

Theologians have no special channel to God, no special certainties, and no final solutions. They know that knowledge is not faith, nor can it produce faith. But they also know knowledge can *nourish* faith. One can know how and why one leans with all one's weight, and who the real person is upon whom they lean.

Theologians are people who love the Church. They love both individuals and the corporate person. Theologians love the people of the Philippines or Ghana, even before meeting them. They love those who are dying, and those who are being born. Just as one loves one's country, one's community, one's tribe, one's people, so too does the theologian love the Church as a corporate person—with all its collective humanity. Unless one loves the Church, one cannot continue to do theology as a ministry. It would then only be a job.

Theologians are ministers. They desire to serve the people of God who ask for this ministry. It requires commitment and responsibility, first to the Lord and then to his people. The ministry functions in many different ways: one studies, writes, lectures, teaches or consults. The theologian acts in different capacities and often is simultaneously a professional teacher, administrator, pastor, bishop, wife or husband. According to the needs of both the Church and the theologian, the way of functioning changes throughout life. Anyone may enter into this field at any time either partially or fully.

The joy, service, and help one can contribute to the journey of others keeps the professional theologian theologizing. To see others find God is reward enough. Being part of this process is a privilege. In the end, theologians know that they remain servants of the Lord. Only God can give God; we simply try to remove every obstacle that hinders this relationship, and promote every contribution that helps it. We want to know if that stranger who comes up behind us and walks with us on our journey is the Lord.

This book has come full circle. It began in experience and

ended in experience. The question "What is theology?" was the point of departure. The building blocks were first laid, then the relationships that make up the content of theology, and finally the tools that a theologian uses. Only in this last chapter did we try to touch the intangible: what is theology to one who does it? After the journey through this book, and reflecting upon the passion involved in theology, if a theologian were asked, "What is theology?", one might not be surprised to hear the answer, "Theology? It is a good and faithful friend."

Charles Hill,

Faith in Search of Understanding :
an introduction to theology,

Dublin : Gill and Macmillan, 1991, pp. 73 - 77

13

Theology, faith, religion, religious education

This book is very much about **faith** — as any theological activity is about faith. There are surely many definitions of **theology**, but, in a nutshell, Anselm's eleventh century one-liner says it all: 'faith seeking understanding'. Karl Rahner, not known for one-liners, defines theology as 'the conscious and methodical explanation and explication of the divine revelation received and grasped in faith'. Both theologians, centuries apart, see theology beginning with faith, whatever of the hypothetical possibility of the non-believing professional 'theologian' making a living writing books on theology or the Bible (not the case with this book, let it be said!). **Religion**, too, is much about faith: it stems from faith and expresses in various forms a relationship born of faith, even if the forms are human and the faith gift divine.

Christian **religious education** is at least basically about faith, in its presuppositions and in some of its intentions and outcomes. This would apply to the various contexts and ages at which it takes place. It can be called faith education, even if its scope may be also to educate about religion and religions. In the history of Christianity, and before it in Judaism, growth in faith was seen related to education and growth in understanding. We have seen Augustine formulating the relationship: 'Seek understanding with a view to faith; have faith with a view to understanding'. And we have examined periods of Christian history, including our own, where an authentic faith response has been retarded through inadequate education in the traditions of Christianity. The Incarnation, which we have taken as paradigm both of Christian gift and Christian response, demands that human effort be made to nourish what has been received from God without that effort.

Faith (and therefore theology) is very much about experience — which is not to say it depends on feelings. We have looked at periods in history when preoccupation with system or attachment to form has kept the believer from tapping into those experiences of God's action (pre-eminently in Jesus) that prompted the faith of the initial believers and shaped the community. At every stage of Christian history, no matter how remote from the time of Jesus, faith has depended on access to those experiences — hence the importance in religious education of continuing that tradition. In the Bible, in the liturgy, in doctrinal and catechetical traditions, in the lived tradition of the community I meet Jesus and become associated with his Paschal Mystery, and my faith is nourished and authenticated. If I express a longing for religious experience of my own, for getting something out of the liturgy, for coming to know the Lord personally, I am looking for nothing more nor less than what brought Paul to faith and made a missioner of him. Faith is, in other words, about story: about my story and Jesus' story, about Paul's story and the community's story; like Paul, and Aquinas, and Luther, and Bultmann, I need to bring my story together with the community's story by experiencing Jesus myself, or my faith withers. Paul met Jesus on the road to Damascus, but he had also to quiz Peter on the community's experience of him (*Galatians* 1:18). Yes, faith and theology (and religious education) are about experience.

Faith is about **revelation**, as Rahner suggested above. The experience of God we receive, directly or dependently, brings us a share in God's self-communication — *koinōnia* in the language of the New Testament. We share in God's own life and what else he has to communicate to us of himself. Such revelation comes to us definitively in Jesus — hence the importance of those traditions that pass that revelatory experience on to us (as we pass it on in religious education). Reading the biblical accounts of God's actions and involving

ourselves in the liturgy should also prove revelatory experiences for us. We are often brought to see God's purposes by the people we meet and the things that happen to us in life's journey, and our faith response is stimulated.

Faith is not about **forms**. Religion, rather, is about forms; faith declares itself in a variety of religious expression, as the Incarnation again requires. Likewise, tradition of the foundational experience involves oral and written records, forms of word in definition, rituals of celebration. But a living faith can outgrow the forms to search for better ones, and attachment to an outmoded, inadequate form can be stifling for faith; prophets from Isaiah onwards have criticised religion for this. The Incarnation teaches us that **change and development** are characteristic of Christian living as of all life; a fundamentalist rejection of new formulas or fresh vision results only in a deadening of faith. Religious education, like the Church generally, must always be searching for contemporary means of articulating the mystery — the vast sacred reality that is the mystery (not the 'puzzle') of Christ.

Likewise, faith is not unaffected by **conditions, cultures, times** — like the man Jesus himself. James in the New Testament ('that epistle of straw', as Luther said in one of his less happy scriptural comments) knew there is little faith education in telling the starving man to 'offer it up' and look towards eternity — something the Church once had a name for. Inhuman conditions are not fertile soil for faith development or any other human development; **humanisation**, liberation was therefore very much Jesus' mission. Matteo Ricci might have been able to be countermanded in his recipe for the conversion of China by the Church of the seventeenth century, but **enculturation** is now accepted as a principle of faith education throughout the Church, if not yet everywhere adopted. A vital Australian Church is likewise committed to a multicultural religious education, aware of cultural groups and oppressed minorities.

We have seen the role of **tradition** in forming faith. A mature faith is the result of keeping in touch with all the traditions of the community of faith, though we have had difficulty down through the ages keeping them all fresh and vital. Only the most recent Council has told Catholics: 'From the table of both the Word of God and the Body of Christ the Church unceasingly receives and offers the bread of life, especially in the sacred liturgy' (*Dogmatic Constitution on Divine Revelation* 21). Keeping in touch with the Church's biblical, liturgical, doctrinal traditions is a demanding **task for religious educators,** as for all believers, but only in that direction lies authentic, mature faith.

Such faith development is clearly **a lifelong task.** Children, of course, are theologising once they begin trying to make sense of what they believe or the community believes, but the questions become more profound and wide-ranging as we grow older in a rapidly changing world. Formation of conscience for responsible use of Christian freedom is also a lengthy process, yet we require it for appreciation of the Christian moral tradition. The Incarnation again suggests that this maturing will not take place without sustained, conscious effort, though the community has not always applied this effort to the benefit of its members after school age. 'Doing theology' is something they need help with throughout life — hence the writing of this little book.

Some relevant reading

Dulles, A., *Models of Revelation*, Doubleday, New York, 1982.

Gascoigne, R., 'The relationship of faith and knowledge', *Word in Life* 35 (1987 February) 8–12.

Miller, D. E., *Story and Context. An Introduction to Christian Education*, Abingdon, Nashville, 1987.

National Catholic Education Commission, *Towards Adult Faith*, NCEC, Melbourne, 1983.

Thornhill, J., 'Handing on the faith', *Word in Life* 35 (1987 May) 5–9.

Vatican II, *Dogmatic Constitution on Divine Revelation*, Rome, 1965.

Exercises in theology

(1) Could you say your study of theology has strengthened your faith, in the way St Augustine saw the relationship of faith and theology? Conversely, do you see how ignorance of theology could retard your faith development? Is the same true of sound religious education and faith, in your experience?

(2) Like Paul, we all have our own spiritual journey, with its peaks and troughs. Trace your own journey, touching on highlights at which an insight into God's purposes has broken through for you. Does it help to place your journey alongside the faith community's, from Paschal Mystery to parousia?

(3) How well equipped are you as an agent of Christian tradition? How well do you know Christianity's biblical tradition? Are you an active participant in its liturgical tradition? Can your students turn to you for an updated statement of Catholic doctrinal tradition? If not, what are you doing about it?

Chapter One

THEOLOGY:
A CRITICAL REFLECTION

Gustavo Gutierrez,

A Theology of Liberation :
history politics and salvation,
revised edition, translated by
Caridad Inda and John Eagleton,

London SCM Press, Ltd.,1988,
pp. 3 - 12, 177 - 182.

Theological reflection—that is, the understanding of the faith—arises spontaneously and inevitably in the believer, in all those who have accepted the gift of the Word of God. Theology is intrinsic to a life of faith seeking to be authentic and complete and is, therefore, essential to the common consideration of this faith in the ecclesial community. There is present in *all believers*—and more so in every Christian community—a rough outline of a theology. There is present an effort to understand the faith, something like a pre-understanding of that faith which is manifested in life, action, and concrete attitude. It is on this foundation, and only because of it, that the edifice of theology—in the precise and technical sense of the term—can be erected. This foundation is not merely a jumping-off point, but the soil into which theological reflection stubbornly and permanently sinks its roots and from which it derives its strength.[1]

But the focus of theological work, in the strict sense of the term, has undergone many transformations throughout the history of the Church. "Bound to the role of the Church, theology is dependent upon its historical development," writes Christian Duquoc.[2] Moreover, as Congar observed recently, this evolution has accelerated to a certain extent in recent years: "The theological work has changed in the past twenty-five years."[3]

THE CLASSICAL TASKS OF THEOLOGY

Theological study has fulfilled different functions throughout the history of the Christian community, but this does not necessarily mean that any of these different approaches has today been definitively superseded. Although expressed in different ways, the essential effort to understand the faith has remained. Moreover, the more penetrating and serious efforts have yielded decisive gains, opening paths along which all subsequent theological reflection must travel. In this perspective it is more accurate to speak of permanent tasks—although they have emerged at different moments in the history of the

Church—than of historically successive stages of theology. Two of these functions are considered classical: theology as wisdom and theology as rational knowledge.

Theology as Wisdom

In the early centuries of the Church, what we now term theology was closely linked to the spiritual life.[4] It was essentially a meditation on the Bible,[5] geared toward spiritual growth. Distinctions were made between the "beginners," the faithful, and the "advanced," who sought perfection.[6] This theology was above all monastic and therefore characterized by a spiritual life removed from worldly concerns;[7] it offered a model for every Christian desirous of advancing along the narrow path of sanctity and seeking a life of spiritual perfection.

Anxious to dialogue with the thought of its time, this theology used Platonic and Neoplatonic categories. In these philosophies it found a metaphysics which stressed the existence of a higher world and the transcendence of an Absolute from which everything came and to which everything returned.[8] The present life, on the other hand, was regarded as essentially contingent and was not valued sufficiently.

It is important to remember, however, that at this same time the reflections of the Greek Fathers on the theology of the world—cosmos and history—go well beyond a mere personal spiritual meditation and place theology in a wider and more fruitful context.

Around the fourteenth century, a rift appears between theologians and masters of the spiritual life. This division can be seen, for example, in such books as *The Imitation of Christ*, which has made a deep impact upon Christian spirituality during past centuries. We are suffering from this dichotomy even today, although it is true that Biblical renewal and the need to reflect upon lay spirituality are providing us with the broad outlines of what might be considered a new spiritual theology.[9]

The spiritual function of theology, so important in the early centuries and later regarded as parenthetical, constitutes, nevertheless, a permanent dimension of theology.[10]

Theology as Rational Knowledge

From the twelfth century on, theology begins to establish itself as a science: "The transition has been made from *sacra pagina* to *theologia* in the modern sense which Abelard . . . was the first to use."[11] The process culminated with Albert the Great and Thomas Aquinas. On the basis of Aristotelian categories, theology was classified as a "subaltern science."[12] St. Thomas's view, nevertheless, was broad and synthetical: theology is not only a science, but also wisdom flowing from the charity which unites a person to God.[13] But this balance is lost when the above-mentioned separation appears between theology and spirituality in the fourteenth century.

The Thomistic idea of science is unclear today because it does not corre-

spond to the definition generally accepted by the modern mind. But the essential feature of St. Thomas Aquinas's work is that theology is an intellectual discipline, born of the meeting of faith and reason.[14] From this point of view, therefore, it is more accurate to regard the theological task not as a science, but as rational knowledge.

The function of theology as rational knowledge is also permanent—insofar as it is a meeting between faith and reason, not exclusively between faith and any one philosophy, nor even between faith and philosophy in general. Reason has, especially today, many other manifestations than philosophical ones. The understanding of the faith is also following along new paths in our day: the social, psychological, and biological sciences. The social sciences, for example, are extremely important for theological reflection in Latin America. Theological thought not characterized by such a rationality and disinterestedness would not be truly faithful to an understanding of the faith.

But it is well to remember, especially with respect to the outdated views which still persist in some quarters, that in Scholastic theology after the thirteenth century there is a degradation of the Thomistic concept of theology.[15] There arises at that time, regardless of outward appearances, a very different way of approaching the theological task. The demands of rational knowledge will be reduced to the need for systematization and clear exposition.[16] Scholastic theology will thus gradually become, especially after the Council of Trent, an ancillary discipline of the magisterium of the Church. Its function will be "(1) to define, present, and explain revealed truths; (2) to examine doctrine, to denounce and condemn false doctrines, and to defend true ones; (3) to teach revealed truths authoritatively."[17]

In summary, theology is of necessity both spirituality and rational knowledge. These are permanent and indispensable functions of all theological thinking. However, both functions must be salvaged, at least partially, from the division and deformations they have suffered throughout history. A reflective outlook and style especially must be retained, rather than one or another specific achievement gained in a historical context different from ours.

THEOLOGY AS CRITICAL REFLECTION ON PRAXIS

The function of theology as critical reflection on praxis has gradually become more clearly defined in recent years, but it has its roots in the first centuries of the Church's life. The Augustinian theology of history which we find in *The City of God,* for example, is based on a true analysis of the signs of the times and the demands with which they challenge the Christian community.

Historical Praxis

For various reasons the existential and active aspects of the Christian life have recently been stressed in a different way than in the immediate past.

In the first place, *charity* has been fruitfully rediscovered as the center of the Christian life. This has led to a more Biblical view of the faith as an act of trust, a going out of one's self, a commitment to God and neighbor, a relationship with others.[18] It is in this sense that St. Paul tells us that faith works through charity: love is the nourishment and the fullness of faith, the gift of one's self to the Other, and invariably to others. This is the foundation of the *praxis* of Christians, of their active presence in history. According to the Bible, faith is the total human response to God, who saves through love.[19] In this light, the understanding of the faith appears as the understanding not of the simple affirmation—almost memorization—of truths, but of a commitment, an over-all attitude, a particular posture toward life.

In a parallel development, Christian *spirituality* has seen a significant evolution. In the early centuries of the Church there emerged the primacy, almost exclusiveness, of a certain kind of contemplative life, hermitical, monastic, characterized by withdrawal from the world, and presented as the model way to sanctity. About the twelfth century the possibility of sharing contemplation by means of preaching and other forms of apostolic activity began to be considered. This point of view was exemplified in the mixed life (contemplative and active) of the mendicant orders and was expressed in the formula: *contemplata aliis tradere* ("to transmit to others the fruits of contemplation").[20] Viewed historically this stage can be considered as a transition to Ignatian spirituality, which sought a difficult but fruitful synthesis between contemplation and action: *in actione contemplativus* ("contemplative in action").[21] This process, strengthened in recent years by the search for a spirituality of the laity, culminates today in the studies on the religious value of the profane and in the spirituality of the activity of the Christian in the world.[22] ✳

Moreover, today there is a greater sensitivity to the *anthropological aspects* of revelation.[23] The Word about God is at the same time a promise to the world. In revealing God to us, the Gospel message reveals us to ourselves in our situation before the Lord and with other humans. The God of Christian revelation is a God incarnate, hence the famous comment of Karl Barth regarding Christian anthropocentrism, "Man is the measure of all things, since God became man."[24] All this has caused the revaluation of human presence and activity in the world, especially in relation to other human beings. On this subject Congar writes: "Seen as a whole, the direction of theological thinking has been characterized by a transference away from attention to the being *per se* of supernatural realities, and toward attention to their relationship with man, with the world, and with the problems and the affirmations of all those who for us represent the *Others*."[25] There is no *horizontalism* in this approach.[26] It is simply a question of the rediscovery of the indissoluble unity of humankind and God.[27]

On the other hand, *the very life of the Church* appears ever more clearly as a *locus theologicus*. Regarding the participation of Christians in the important social movements of their time, Chenu wrote insightfully more than thirty years ago: "They are active *loci theologici* for the doctrines of grace, the

Incarnation, and the redemption, as expressly promulgated and described in detail by the papal encyclicals. They are poor theologians who, wrapped up in their manuscripts and scholastic disputations, are not open to these amazing events, not only in the pious fervor of their hearts but formally in their science; there is a theological datum and an extremely fruitful one, in the *presence* of the Spirit."[28] The so-called new theology attempted to adopt this posture some decades ago. The fact that the life of the Church is a source for all theological analysis has been recalled to mind often since then. The Word of God gathers and is incarnated in the community of faith, which gives itself to the service of all.

Vatican Council II has strongly reaffirmed the idea of a Church of service and not of power. This is a Church which is not centered upon itself and which does not "find itself" except when it "loses itself," when it lives "the joys and the hopes, the griefs and the anxieties of persons of this age" (*Gaudium et spes*, no. 1). All of these trends provide a new focus for seeing the presence and activity of the Church in the world as a starting point for theological reflection.

What since John XXIII and Vatican Council II began to be called a theology of the *signs of the times*[29] can be characterized along the same lines, although this takes a step beyond narrow ecclesial limits. It must not be forgotten that the signs of the times are not only a call to intellectual analysis. They are above all a call to pastoral activity, to commitment, and to service. Studying the signs of the times includes both dimensions. Therefore, *Gaudium et spes*, no. 44, points out that discerning the signs of the times is the responsibility of every Christian, especially pastors and theologians, to hear, distinguish, and interpret the many voices of our age, and to judge them in the light of the divine Word. In this way, revealed truths can always be more deeply penetrated, better understood, and set forth to greater advantage. Attributing this role to every member of the People of God and singling out the pastors—charged with guiding the activity of the Church—highlights the call to commitment which the signs of the times imply. Necessarily connected with this consideration, the function of theologians will be to afford greater clarity regarding this commitment by means of intellectual analysis. (It is interesting to note that the inclusion of theologians in the above-mentioned text met opposition during the conciliar debates.)

Another factor, this time of a *philosophical* nature, reinforces the importance of human action as the point of departure for all reflection. The philosophical issues of our times are characterized by new relationships of humankind with nature, born of advances in science and technology. These new bonds affect the awareness that persons have of themselves and of their active relationships with others.

Maurice Blondel, moving away from an empty and fruitless spirituality and attempting to make philosophical speculation more concrete and alive, presented it as a critical reflection on action. This reflection attempts to understand the internal logic of an action through which persons seek fulfillment by constantly transcending themselves.[30] Blondel thus contributed to the elaboration of a new *apologetics* and became one of the most important thinkers of contemporary theology, including the most recent trends.

To these factors can be added the influence of *Marxist thought*, focusing on praxis and geared to the transformation of the world.[31] The Marxist influence began to be felt in the middle of the nineteenth century, but in recent times its cultural impact has become greater. Many agree with Sartre that "Marxism, as the formal framework of all contemporary philosophical thought, cannot be superseded."[32] Be that as it may, contemporary theology does in fact find itself in direct and fruitful confrontation with Marxism, and it is to a large extent due to Marxism's influence that theological thought, searching for its own sources, has begun to reflect on the meaning of the transformation of this world and human action in history.[33] Further, this confrontation helps theology to perceive what its efforts at understanding the faith receive from the historical praxis of humankind in history as well as what its own reflection might mean for the transformation of the world.

Finally, the rediscovery of the *eschatological dimension* in theology has also led us to consider the central role of historical praxis. Indeed, if human history is above all else an opening to the future, then it is a task, a political occupation, through which we orient and open ourselves to the gift which gives history its transcendent meaning: the full and definitive encounter with the Lord and with other humans. "To do the truth," as the Gospel says, thus acquires a precise and concrete meaning in terms of the importance of action in Christian life. Faith in a God who loves us and calls us to the gift of full communion with God and fellowship with others not only is not foreign to the transformation of the world; it leads necessarily to the building up of that fellowship and communion in history. Moreover, only by doing this truth will our faith be "verified," in the etymological sense of the word. From this notion has recently been derived the term *orthopraxis*, which still disturbs the sensitivities of some. The intention, however, is not to deny the meaning of *orthodoxy*, understood as a proclamation of and reflection on statements considered to be true. Rather, the goal is to balance and even to reject the primacy and almost exclusiveness which doctrine has enjoyed in Christian life and above all to modify the emphasis, often obsessive, upon the attainment of an orthodoxy which is often nothing more than fidelity to an obsolete tradition or a debatable interpretation. In a more positive vein, the intention is to recognize the work and importance of concrete behavior, of deeds, of action, of praxis in the Christian life.[34] "And this, it seems to me, has been the greatest transformation which has taken place in the Christian conception of existence," said Edward Schillebeeckx in an interview. "It is evident that thought is also necessary for action. But the Church has for centuries devoted its attention to formulating truths and meanwhile did almost nothing to better the world. In other words, the Church focused on orthodoxy and left orthopraxis in the hands of nonmembers and nonbelievers."[35]

In the last analysis, this concern for praxis seeks to avoid the practices which

gave rise to Bernanos' sarcastic remark: "God does not choose the same ones to keep his Word as to fulfill it."[36]

Critical Reflection

All the factors we have considered have been responsible for a more accurate understanding that communion with the Lord inescapably means a Christian life centered around a concrete and creative commitment of service to others. They have likewise led to the rediscovery or explicit formulation of the function of theology as critical reflection. It would be well at this point to define further our terms.

Theology must be critical reflection on humankind, on basic human principles. Only with this approach will theology be a serious discourse, aware of itself, in full possession of its conceptual elements. But we are not referring exclusively to this epistemological aspect when we talk about theology as critical reflection. We also refer to a clear and critical attitude regarding economic and socio-cultural issues in the life and reflection of the Christian community. To disregard these is to deceive both oneself and others. But above all, we intend this term to express the theory of a definite practice. Theological reflection would then necessarily be a criticism of society and the Church insofar as they are called and addressed by the Word of God; it would be a critical theory, worked out in the light of the Word accepted in faith and inspired by a practical purpose—and therefore indissolubly linked to historical praxis.[37]

By preaching the Gospel message, by its sacraments, and by the charity of its members, the Church proclaims and shelters the gift of the Kingdom of God in the heart of human history.[38] The Christian community professes a "faith which works through charity." It is—at least ought to be—real charity, action, and commitment to the service of others. Theology is reflection, a critical attitude. Theology *follows*; it is the second step.[39] What Hegel used to say about philosophy can likewise be applied to theology: it rises only at sundown. The pastoral activity of the Church does not flow as a conclusion from theological premises. Theology does not produce pastoral activity; rather it reflects upon it. Theology must be able to find in pastoral activity the presence of the Spirit inspiring the action of the Christian community.[40]

A privileged *locus theologicus* for understanding the faith will be the life, preaching, and historical commitment of the Church.[41]

To reflect upon the presence and action of the Christian in the world means, moreover, to go beyond the visible boundaries of the Church. This is of prime importance. It implies openness to the world, gathering the questions it poses, being attentive to its historical transformations. In the words of Congar, "If the Church wishes to deal with the real questions of the modern world and to attempt to respond to them, . . . it must open as it were a new chapter of theologico-pastoral epistemology. Instead of using only revelation and tradition as starting points, as classical theology has generally done, it must start with facts and questions derived from the world and from history." It is precisely this opening to the totality of human history that allows theology to fulfill its critical function vis-à-vis ecclesial praxis without narrowness.

This critical task is indispensable. Reflection in the light of faith must constantly accompany the pastoral action of the Church. By keeping historical events in their proper perspective, theology helps safeguard society and the Church from regarding as permanent what is only temporary. Critical reflection thus always plays the inverse role of an ideology which rationalizes and justifies a given social and ecclesial order. On the other hand, theology, by pointing to the sources of revelation, helps to orient pastoral activity; it puts it in a wider context and so helps it to avoid activism and immediatism. Theology as critical reflection thus fulfills a liberating function for humankind and the Christian community, preserving them from fetishism and idolatry, as well as from a pernicious and belittling narcissism. Understood in this way, theology has a necessary and permanent role in liberation from every form of religious alienation—which is often fostered by the ecclesiastical institution itself when it impedes an authentic approach to the Word of the Lord.

As critical reflection on society and the Church, theology is an understanding which both grows and, in a certain sense, changes. If the commitment of the Christian community in fact takes different forms throughout history, the understanding which accompanies the vicissitudes of this commitment will be constantly renewed and will take untrodden paths. A theology which has as its points of reference only "truths" which have been established once and for all—and not the Truth which is also the Way—can be only static and, in the long run, sterile. In this sense the often-quoted and misinterpreted words of Bouillard take on new validity: "A theology which is not up-to-date is a false theology."[43]

Finally, theology thus understood, that is to say as linked to praxis, fulfills a prophetic function insofar as it interprets historical events with the intention of revealing and proclaiming their profound meaning. According to Cullmann, this is the meaning of the prophetic role: "The prophet does not limit himself as does the fortune-teller to isolated revelations, but his prophecy becomes preaching, proclamation. He explains to the people the true meaning of all events; he informs them of the plan and will of God at the particular moment."[44] But if theology is based on this observation of historical events and contributes to the discovery of their meaning, it is with the purpose of making Christians' commitment within them more radical and clear. Only with the exercise of the prophetic function understood in this way, will the theologian be—to borrow an expression from Antonio Gramsci—a new kind of "organic intellectual."[45] Theologians will be personally and vitally engaged in historical realities with specific times and places. They will be engaged where nations, social classes, and peoples struggle to free themselves from domination and oppression by other nations, classes, and peoples. In the last analysis, the true interpretation of the meaning revealed by theology is achieved only in historical praxis. "The hermeneutics of the Kingdom of God," observed Schillebeeckx,

"consists especially in making the world a better place. Only in this way will I be able to discover what the Kingdom of God means."[46] We have here a political hermeneutics of the Gospel.[47]

CONCLUSION

Theology as a critical reflection on Christian praxis in the light of the Word does not replace the other functions of theology, such as wisdom and rational knowledge; rather it presupposes and needs them. But this is not all. We are not concerned here with a mere juxtaposition. The critical function of theology necessarily leads to redefinition of these other two tasks. Henceforth, wisdom and rational knowledge will more explicitly have ecclesial praxis as their point of departure and their context. It is in reference to this praxis that an understanding of spiritual growth based on Scripture should be developed, and it is through this same praxis that faith encounters the problems posed by human reason. Given the theme of the present work, we will be especially aware of this critical function of theology with the ramifications suggested above. This approach will lead us to pay special attention to the life of the Church and to commitments which Christians, impelled by the Spirit and in communion with others, undertake in history. We will give special consideration to participation in the process of liberation, an outstanding phenomenon of our times, which takes on special meaning in the so-called Third World countries.

This kind of theology, arising from concern with a particular set of issues, will perhaps give us the solid and permanent albeit modest foundation for the *theology in a Latin American perspective* which is both desired and needed. This Latin American focus would not be due to a frivolous desire for originality, but rather to a fundamental sense of historical efficacy and also—why hide it?—to the desire to contribute to the life and reflection of the universal Christian community. But in order to make our contribution, this desire for universality—as well as input from the Christian community as a whole—must be present from the beginning. To concretize this desire would be to overcome particularistic tendencies—provincial and chauvinistic—and produce something *unique*, both particular and universal, and therefore fruitful.[48]

"The only future that theology has, one might say, is to become the theology of the future," Harvey Cox has said.[49] But this theology of the future must necessarily be a critical appraisal of historical praxis, of the historical task in the sense we have attempted to sketch. Moltmann says that theological concepts "do not limp after reality . . . . They illuminate reality by displaying its future."[50] In our approach, to reflect critically on the praxis of liberation is to "limp after" reality. The present in the praxis of liberation, in its deepest dimension, is pregnant with the future; hope must be an inherent part of our present commitment in history. Theology does not initiate this future which exists in the present. It does not create the vital attitude of hope out of nothing. Its role is more modest. It interprets and explains these as the true underpinnings of history. To reflect upon a forward-directed action is not to concentrate on the past. It does not mean being the caboose of the present. Rather it is to penetrate the present reality, the movement of history, that which is driving history toward the future. To reflect on the basis of the historical praxis of liberation is to reflect in the light of the future which is believed in and hoped for. It is to reflect with a view to action which transforms the present. But it does not mean doing this from an armchair; rather it means sinking roots where the pulse of history is beating at this moment and illuminating history with the Word of the Lord of history, who irreversibly committed himself to the present moment of humankind to carry it to its fulfillment.

It is for all these reasons that the theology of liberation offers us not so much a new theme for reflection as a *new way* to do theology. Theology as critical reflection on historical praxis is a liberating theology, a theology of the liberating transformation of the history of humankind and also therefore that part of humankind—gathered into *ecclesia*—which openly confesses Christ. This is a theology which does not stop with reflecting on the world, but rather tries to be part of the process through which the world is transformed. It is a theology which is open—in the protest against trampled human dignity, in the struggle against the plunder of the vast majority of humankind, in liberating love, and in the building of a new, just, and comradely society—to the gift of the Kingdom of God.

Chapter 9

REASON AND REVELATION

Marianne H. Micks
Introduction to Theology
revised edition
New York : The Seabury Press, 1983
pp. 91 - 101, 167 - 168.

"I solemnly swear to tell the truth, the whole truth, and nothing but the truth, so help me God." Have you ever stopped to analyze this familiar oath? On critical inspection the words appear so pretentious as to be absurd. In order that the jury may establish what truly happened, the witness promises to tell the whole truth. Where was he last August 1? On a universal scale, he has no idea. He has been whirling through space for a month since then. Would the jury care to be reminded of this fact?

And is it a fact? In the courtroom setting, hearsay evidence is out of order. The witness's senses tell him that the earth beneath him is flat and motionless; but sensory data are notoriously deceptive. In spite of the conflict with his everyday experience, he has accepted the evidence of scientists who tell him that the earth is constantly moving. So he knows that he does not know the whole answer.

The oath charges him, furthermore, to call on God to help him tell the truth. But does he know enough about deity to know whether it is of such a nature that it could offer help in truth-telling? Is it capable of this sort of personalized interest in what anyone says? How does he know? If he took the words he recited literally, a scrupulous witness might well find himself tongue-tied.

Very few people today would ever volunteer to speak the whole truth. We are more modest in our claims to knowledge. Yet many still value the idea of truth and try to know and tell it. If they reflect about it, they are confronted by serious questions. How does anyone know anything? Do we live in a rational universe, where it makes sense to speak of knowing the truth at all? Is it a whole, or are there just relative truths, so that one should speak only of scientific truth, or of psychological truth, or of religious truth? Should theologians perhaps dismiss any truth claim whatsoever, on the grounds that truth is a religiously irrelevant concept?

Such questions are independent of any formal concern for epistemology. They arise from the complexity of the scientific age in which we live. The spirit of that age makes it impossible for many people to accept the idea that there is any intelligible, unitary meaning in the cosmos. Ever since Galileo burst the bonds of a tidy, self-contained universe, men and women have found it increasingly difficult to entertain the notion that we live in a world governed by reason. Ever since Freud unveiled the subconscious, the doubts have grown stronger. The truly modern person, it has been said, is one who believes in the ultimate irrationality of everything.[1] Philosophers as different as Bertrand Russell and Jean-Paul Sartre share the conviction that the universe is completely indifferent to human beings and their values, including the value of truth. By definition, the Christian has rejected this belief; therefore he or she is faced with two other problems—the problem of relating science to religion, and the concomitant problem of authority.

OUR APPROACHES TO KNOWLEDGE

Because the question of science and religion is usually posed in a false form, believers today (professional scientists as well as professional theologians) tend to deny vehemently the existence of a conflict between them. Too vehemently. Unless one is a biblical literalist, it is easy to demonstrate that there is no necessary abyss between established facts of geology, say, and the creation story of Genesis 1, or between theories of evolution and the story of Adam. But beyond this elementary level, a genuine conflict remains for most Christians. They are committed, on the one hand, to the concept that revelation provides trustworthy knowledge about ultimate reality. They are taught such respect for the scientific method, on the other hand, that

it easily assumes exclusive rights to the province of human reason. Since neither God nor Santa Claus is subject to empirical verification, modern people almost inevitably put them in the same class. Religion, they conclude, is the province of faith (usually qualified as blind), whereas knowledge is the product of scientific inquiry.

If one takes a second look at this conclusion, one must quickly acknowledge that it oversimplifies. In all areas of human knowing there is an element of faith. The presuppositions of both science and religion are beyond proof in the sense of laboratory demonstration. And in both science and religion one must trust reports of others. Much of what we call scientific knowledge is at odds with our own experience. We have time and talent to verify only a very small part of it by our own experimental investigation. For the most part, we merely trust the testimony of the experts. A revealed religion such as Christianity also offers alleged knowledge of reality, some of which is subject to experiential verification and some of which is not. But it is not self-evident how the two types of knowledge fit together. Is all truth of a piece?

Deep-seated individualism leads many Americans to distrust authoritarianism, and to confuse it with authority. Rejecting the former, they fail to see the necessity for the latter. The question of authority, indeed, has been well dubbed the Achilles heel of Protestantism.[2] Religious certainty, like any other certainty, poses a problem of authority. What sources of knowledge are genuinely trustworthy? How should a thinking Christian combine the evidence of personal experience with the experience of others? What weight is to be given to human reason? What weight is to be given to the Bible? What place to a teaching Church?

Contemporary Christianity thinks about reason and revelation in at least four different ways. Although the terms in which the problem was posed were slightly different, the relationship between reason and revelation was also one of the central intellectual concerns of the twelfth and thirteenth centuries; and theologians then took the same four approaches. In thinking about knowledge of the truth, some Christian believers in both ages have settled for suppressing one source of knowledge. This answer has two forms. One gives major authority to revelation and lets reason say what it will, unheeded. The other gives major authority to reason and puts revelation in the back seat, to support rational conclusions as and when it can. The third and fourth ways both attempt to synthesize reason and revelation; but the third calls for a division of labor between them, assigning different but complementary functions to each. The fourth gives primacy to faith in all knowing, but considers reason a necessary partner with revelation in a joint search for knowledge.

REASON VS. REVELATION

The authority of the Church was undoubtedly a presupposition of the age we call medieval, but its theologians were intensely aware that Church authority could be questioned. Within that united Christendom which we are so prone to romanticize, three developments contributed to making them acutely conscious, in the twelfth and thirteenth centuries, of problems of reason and revelation. The first was renewed contact with another revealed religion. Although the Moslem advance into Europe had been decisively halted in the eighth century, Spain remained largely under Islamic control for the next three hundred years. With the capture of Toledo at the end of the eleventh century, the first great step was made in the Christian reconquest of Spain. By the end of the thirteenth century, Moslem territory had shrunk to the little coastal emirate of Granada. In the same period, the Crusades brought fresh encounters with Islam in the East, and fresh need to assert the truth of the Christian revelation as over against the revelation vouchsafed to the prophet Mohammed and embodied in the Qur'an.

Meanwhile the rise of the schools, and then of the universities, in Europe produced a growing body of human knowledge, and with it a growing desire to relate theology to other intellectual disciplines. The schoolmen exerted a conscious effort to make theology scientific. They sought to apply the principles of logic to the truths of revelation, to sharpen rational analysis of what the Church proposed for a Christian's belief.

And in the twelfth century, Christian Europe rediscovered Aristotle. Although his logic had been known all along, through the works of Boethius, the rest of Aristotelian thought first came to Latin Christians by way of the Islamic scholars in the Spanish universities. For such scholars, Aristotle created a sharp conflict between reason

and revelation. What was one to do when Aristotle's conclusions seemed to contradict the Qur'an? In his treatise on *The Agreement of Religion and Philosophy*, the great Moslem philosopher Averroes explored the problem and decided that, for the philosopher only, the necessary demonstrations of reason are compelling, but that the philosopher is under no obligation to disturb the faith of common people for whom the materials of revelation provide sufficient certainty.[3]

When the Christian intellectuals made Aristotle "The Philosopher," they encountered the same problem, and some of them came to the same conclusion. Aristotle taught them, for example, that the world was eternal. Revelation taught them that it was created out of nothing "in the beginning." Some theologians at the University of Paris, confronted with two seeming irreconcilables, decided that they need not be harmonized. There can be such a thing as necessary conclusions from philosophy, they thought, which do not gibe with "the truth of God." The theories of these Latin Averroists, which led eventually to Church condemnation of the study of Aristotle, provide an extreme example of a divorce between revelation and reason.

More representative of the age, and of the parallel positions in the modern world, are two major antagonists in the twelfth-century Church, Bernard of Clairvaux and Peter Abelard. In the conflict between them, Bernard is the great advocate of revelation, against Abelard, disciple of reason. Neither man wanted a complete divorce between reason and revelation, but each resolved tension in the marriage by giving one partner chief authority.

Christian believers who accept revelation unquestioningly have the simplest answer to the problem we are considering. As Etienne Gilson expresses it, they merely say, "since God has spoken to us, it is no longer necessary for us to think."[4] Bernard (1091–1153) shares some of this spirit, but it would be a mistake to dismiss him simply as a credulous antiintellectual. He was not opposed to thought, but he was more concerned with action and with contemplation. As an activist, Bernard is said to have carried the twelfth century on his shoulders. When one weighs his reform of monastic life, his preaching of the Second Crusade, his diplomatic work to heal the papal schism, his fight against the new form of Manicheanism in southern France, along with his efforts to silence Peter Abelard, the description seems an apt one. As a contemplative and a mystic, Bernard

was a man overwhelmed by the humility of love. He was utterly convinced that the way that leads to truth is Christ, and that the way that leads to Christ is humility.[5] To Bernard, meditation on the name of Jesus Christ was worth more than a thousand theological disputations.

Small wonder then that Bernard, who believed in mounting to truth by the way of humility, was shocked and disturbed by the arrogance of Peter Abelard. Abelard, the brilliant lecturer in theology at the University of Paris, had "the intelligence that would reach down a handful of stars from heaven and set them by his book to read by."[6] To Bernard he was a "a man who does not know his own limitations, making void the virtue of the cross by the cleverness of his words."[7] The Abbot of Clairvaux was always opposed to leaning too much on human reasoning.

Bernard was so disturbed by the critical spirit which Abelard was engendering in the Church that he agreed to personal debate with him before a council of bishops at Sens in 1140. Before and after that council, he wrote numerous letters denouncing the errors of his opponent. He has fault to find with certain specific doctrines, but it is Abelard's general approach to theology that is the real root of the problem as Bernard sees it. Writing to his friend Cardinal Haimeric, the abbot complains that Abelard "tries to explore with his reason what the devout mind grasps at once with a vigorous faith. Faith believes, it does not dispute. But this man, apparently holding God suspect, will not believe anything until he has first examined it with his reason."[8]

Reporting to Pope Innocent after Sens, he charges that Abelard "insults the Doctors of the Church by holding up the philosophers for exaggerated praises. He prefers their ideas and his own novelties to the doctrines of faith and the Catholic Fathers."[9] Bernard clearly believes that the faith was once for all delivered to the saints and has been cherished by the Church ever since. This should be enough to satisfy even Abelard. But instead,

> ... mere human ingenuity is taking on itself to solve everything, and leave nothing to faith. It is trying for things above itself, prying into things too strong for it, rushing into divine things, and profaning rather than re-

vealing what is holy. Things closed and sealed, it is not opening but tearing asunder, and what it is not able to force open, that it considers to be of no account and not worthy of belief.[10]

Peter Abelard (1079–1142) was definitely not satisfied with the received faith. His approach to revelation is summed up in the title of one of his best-known works, *Sic et Non*. He knew full well that the Bible and the fathers answer yes and no to the questions asked of them; he collected their conflicting testimony to demonstrate the problem. "Here begin sentences taken from the Holy Scriptures which seem opposed to each other..." *Sic et Non* starts out.[11] There follow over 150 theological questions answered both ways. Yet Abelard was not rejecting the idea of revelation. He did not substitute the dogma of God's total silence, as a modern rationalist might, leaving human minds with only a rumor about ultimate being. He was not recanting under pressure from authority when he wrote, "I do not want to be a philosopher at the price of being rejected by Paul; not yet an Aristotle at the price of being rejected by Christ, for there is no other name under heaven whereby I can be saved."[12]

What was he trying to do then? No one could answer the question better than Helen Waddell has done in her unforgettable novel *Peter Abelard*. She re-creates the moment when the idea for *Sic et Non* is born, as Abelard remembers the teachers he has studied under and triumphed over:

> Sheep every one of them, with their meek faces, browsing over and over the old close-bitten pastures, with their "St. Augustine saith ... St. Jerome saith ... The Blessed Gregory saith..." As if one could not prove anything, and deny it, and prove it back again, out of St. Augustine alone. Sometime he would do it, for a testimony unto them. Pit the Fathers one against the other. Smash the whole blind system of authority and substitute ... Master Peter Abelard? said the mocking voice within him. He shook his head, suddenly humble. Not that. Not that. But a reasonable soul. *The spirit of man is the candle of the Lord.* Abelard shuddered and was

still. It was about him again, the dark immensity, the pressure of some greatness from without upon his brain, and that within which struggled to break through to it. *I said, Ye are gods.*[13]

Where the evidence of scripture and tradition conflicted, Abelard believed that we are to use our God-given reason in judgment. For it was because of reason, as Abelard understood it, that we are said to be made in the image of God.

Bernard's distrust of reason and his confidence in revelation put him close to naive believers of today who seem to equate revelation with a long-distance telephone call from God. Abelard's honest facing of the conflicts in scripture and tradition is a necessary corrective to this fideism, and a treasured witness to the art of Christian doubt. But his great trust in the capacity of the human mind is difficult to share in an age which knows as much as ours about individual rationalization and communal brainwashing. The remaining two ideas which Christians have held and still hold about the relation between reason and revelation take the limitations of both more fully into account. The medieval spokesman for the first is Thomas Aquinas; for the second, Anselm of Canterbury.

ASSENT THROUGH SCIENCE AND FAITH

No man's thought ever fits as neatly into a pigeonhole as his interpreters would like. Even Thomas Aquinas (1225–1274), one of the most consistent and systematic thinkers known to Christian history, defies efforts to label him once and for all. His eucharistic hymns, for example, call into question all unqualified statements that he achieves a completely balanced synthesis of reason and revelation. Nevertheless, in his systematic works he speaks with clarity and finality for a division of labor between them. Science and faith, Thomas believed, are two specifically different kinds of assent.[14]

Defenders of this position in the modern world want to distinguish spheres of religion and science by clear definition of their respective roles. In a letter printed in a popular magazine some years ago, a Jewish scientist argued that science does not require our belief in any statements except those that report direct sense perceptions, and

that it cannot command our disbelief on matters outside its stated field.[15] Surprised as the writer might be with the designation, this is the voice of a Thomist in the twentieth century. For to Thomas Aquinas, faith is assent of the intellect to that which the intellect does not see to be true. *Scientia*, knowledge, is assent to what the intellect does see to be true, ultimately on the basis of sensory perception.

Gilson pictures a Thomist as "a man who does not like to believe what he can know, and who never pretends to know what can be believed."[16] In support of a separation between the stated fields of science and religion, our modern Thomist went on to say that religion, of course, need not be irrelevant to the scientist. The original Thomist agreed. His word portrait is finished, therefore, with the qualification "... and yet a man whose faith and knowledge grow into an organic unity because they both spring from the same divine source."[17]

Today as in the day of the master, Thomists rest on the principle of noncontradiction. Knowledge which comes from science, and beliefs from revelation, are parts of one whole truth of God. Both are necessary. In his *Summa*, directed especially to the Moslem intellectuals— translated today under the title *On the Truth of the Catholic Faith*[18] —Thomas spells out with precision the distinction between natural reason and revelation. He is writing theology; and although theology is a science whose conclusions necessarily follow from its principles, those principles are articles of faith. So, for that matter, are the first principles of all sciences, in Thomas's opinion. Nevertheless, some true knowledge about God is available to natural reason.

Thomas divides his work into two distinct parts—the first dealing with truths which faith proposes and reason investigates, the second dealing with truths of faith above reason, for which reason can bring forth probable but not demonstrable arguments. Reason, in Thomas's mind, can tell a person that God is, and a great deal about what God does. It can also tell a person about the human beings God creates, and about their meaning and purpose. But it can never enable a person to reach his or her proper end, to fulfill his or her true purpose. For that, the vision of God, revelation, is absolutely necessary. Only through revelation can anyone come to believe the saving truth of a triune God incarnate in Jesus Christ, whose means of grace are given through the sacraments of his Church. Such truth, however, is not opposed to reason, even though reason can never demonstate it conclusively.

In Thomas's system, reason and revelation form a perfectly matched couple. They complement each other every step of the way. Even as reason supports revelation in its sphere, by bringing forth probable arguments in favor of facts which are originally beyond its grasp, so revelation assists reason in its province. Under the right conditions, human reason *can* discover many things about God, but only a few intellectuals have the capacity and the time to use it for this purpose. And even their conclusions could be mixed with error.[19] The Word of God, to which faith assents, makes up for these deficiencies of natural reason. So, for Thomas, there is complete harmony between reason and revelation, but in the end revelation does most of the work.

FAITH LEADING TO REASON

Our fourth and final representative almost tips the balance of responsibility in the opposite direction. Anselm (1033–1109), who reluctantly became Archbishop of Canterbury in 1093, was the first great theologian of the Middle Ages. His starting place was faith. With Augustine, he was convinced that unless you believe you will not be able to understand. Therefore the watchword of Anselm's position is *Credo ut intelligam*. I believe *in order that* . . . Anselm's faith is always a faith seeking understanding.

It was in search of understanding that Anselm launched into the intellectual exercise for which he is most widely known, his celebrated ontological proof for the existence of God. It is found in his *Proslogion*, which bears the subtitle *Fides Quaerens Intellectum*. Just what Anselm achieved with his logical argument (that, as "that than which nothing greater can be conceived," God must necessarily exist) is a matter of debate. Some interpreters insist that he was not trying to prove anything; he was simply meditating on divine being, trying to show what is implicit in that very notion. Despite various efforts to rehabilitate Anselm's argument, the sympathies of most lay theologians remain with Anselm's first critic, Gaunilon the Fool. Gaunilon retorted that he could conceive of a perfect island in the Atlantic, but that the reality of such an island did not follow merely from his having an idea of it.

For our purposes, the important thing is not the validity of the argument, but the fact of it. Anselm knew that philosophical dialectic was not the source of faith, but he believed it was a useful and even beautiful instrument in the service of faith. Reason (which is essentially logic for Anselm) functions in the context of faith; but it must function. To seek understanding is part of the nature of faith. Just because we possess the certainty of faith, we must hunger after a reason for the faith that is in us.

Anselm's attitude toward revelation and reason had a decisive influence on one of the most profound and prolific twentieth-century theologians, Karl Barth. In the preface to his study of Anselm, Barth declares that it is "a vital key, if not the key" to understanding of the whole process of thought in his monumental *Church Dogmatics*.[20] Barth explains that we approach Anselm's position when we say that, by its very nature, faith desires knowledge. "*Credo ut intelligam* means: It is my very faith itself that summons me to knowledge."[21] For Anselm, the God in whom we have faith is Truth itself, and the author of all that we call truth apart from him. From his way of relating reason and revelation, it follows that the faithful use reason fully, in order that they may have joy in their believing.

In all ages some Christians have joined Bernard of Clairvaux in believing the authority of the Bible and the Church, no matter how absurd revealed truth might seem to the human intellect. In all ages some Christians have joined Peter Abelard in doubt of this authority. Since God has given human beings minds, they believe, they should use them in rigorous critique of any proposition that seems unreasonable. With Anselm and Aquinas, other Christians cannot be content with any sort of intellectual schizophrenia. They are drawn to seek wholeness. Many today are convinced, with Thomas, that there can be no final contradiction between the knowledge acquired by natural reason and the supranatural truth revealed by God. Less confident than Anselm that all the truths of revelation can be demonstrated by logic, many others today start in faith nevertheless, on a lifelong search for understanding.

CHAPTER 9 / REASON AND REVELATION

1. W. T. Stace, "Man Against Darkness," *Atlantic*, September 1948, p. 55.

2. Robert McAfee Brown, *The Spirit of Protestantism* (New York: Oxford University Press, 1961), ch. 14.

3. This and the following paragraph are dependent on Etienne Gilson, *Reason and Revelation in the Middle Ages* (New York: Charles Scribner's Sons, 1948), ch. 2.

4. Ibid., p. 6.

5. Etienne Gilson, *History of Christian Philosophy in the Middle Ages* (New York: Random House, 1955), p. 164.

6. Helen Waddell, *Peter Abelard* (New York: The Viking Press; Compass Books ed., 1959), p. 38.

7. Bruno Scott James (tr.), *The Letters of St. Bernard of Clairvaux* (Chicago: Henry Regnery Co., 1953), p. 321.

8. Ibid., p. 328.

9. Ibid., p. 318.

10. Ibid., p. 316.

11. As quoted by James, ibid., p. 316, n. 4.

12. As quoted by James, ibid., p. 314.

13. Waddell, op. cit., p. 6.

14. Gilson, *Reason and Revelation*, p. 73.

15. Herbert Goldstein, president, Association of Orthodox Jewish Scientists, in "Letters to the Editor," *Saturday Review*, May 4, 1963, p. 21.

16. Gilson, *Reason and Revelation*, p. 83.

17. Ibid., p. 84.

18. Anton C. Pegis (tr.), *Summa Contra Gentiles* (New York: Image Books, 1955), vols. I–IV.

19. Ibid., Book I, Ch. 4.

20. Karl Barth, *Anselm: Fides Quaerens Intellectum* (New York: Meridian Books, 1962), p. 11.

21. Ibid., p. 18.

J. J. Mueller
<u>What is Theology ?</u>
Wilmington, Delaware : Michael Glazier, Inc., 1988
pp. 33 - 40.

C. FAITH

The third and final building block of theological anthropology is the pursuit of good. In gospel terms, this is called "faith." It relates the human person to the goal of life by overcoming sin. If we think of sin as a downward pull (hell), salvation as an upward pull (heaven), then faith is a forward movement toward salvation (this world and its history). While the concept of faith is simple to understand, the way it functions becomes more complicated and nuanced throughout the history of Judaism and Christianity. Let us begin with the basic concept as it comes from experience and then examine its implications for theology.

The word faith comes from the Hebrew word "emet" which means "to lean on something with all one's weight." The word was used to describe the solid support which held something up. For example, when people of the sandy desert built a house, unless it was built upon something solid like rock, the shifting sand would destroy the house. Faith implied the building of anything upon a solid foundation. In the scriptures, God was often called a rock: "my rock, my salvation"; "my fortress, my rock"; "rock of ages." Jesus finished his sermon on the mountain with a parable of the wise person, in this case the disciple, who built his house upon the firm foundation of rock. To have faith meant that one leaned with all one's weight upon the rock of God who was solid and would not allow one to fall.

People also used the experience of human relationships to explain faith. For example, faith described the experience of a mother holding her baby in her arms. The baby is secure, where she wants to be, comforted, solid. If the baby is taken away from the mother, the baby cries. What is more, Mom won't drop the baby. So too is it with God. Faith means that we rest in the loving embrace of God our parent without fear of being taken, falling, or feeling insecure. God holds each of us solidly. This meaning extends outward to others, e.g. in times of trouble one leans upon a true friend knowing one will not be let down. Faith describes what is solid; the foundation of human life is God and we lean upon him with all our weight.

This same word "emet" has another important derivation. It is the same stem that forms the word "truth." That God is our rock, our solidity and that of the world, is the most basic truth of all creation. To place oneself in God's arms by faith is to make the correct decision, the most truthful act imaginable. Just as a true friend won't let us down, so with God. Our faith is correctly placed in the solid bedrock of truth. Such solidity brings with it the harmony and peace that creation intended. Thus faith describes the basic relation of humanity to God and functions as an important building block for other theological concepts.

If we return to the story of Adam and Eve, humanity broke the correct relationship with God. And with the break, we no longer saw God face to face in intimate friendship. Interestingly, God does not leave the garden and depart for heaven, thereby removing himself from the world. God remains in the garden. It is Adam and Eve who leave, thereby removing themselves from intimacy with God. From this day on, humans will not see God directly. God is hidden from our sight and we are removed from his presence. However, God may elect to be with us outside the garden. Notice that in either case, God remains in this world. Genesis leaves us with a truth that humanity will subsequently

live with: we must relate to God as a hidden God. Faith, then refers to what we cannot see but must trust anyway. In sum, life is an act of faith, which is trust. Problems are encountered because, when we cannot see God, we do not know exactly how to relate with him, what to say or do, what he wants for us, whether he is watching us, whether he cares for us. While Genesis describes only Judeo-Christian anthropology, these concerns pervade all religious beliefs.

The re-establishment of the relation with God, then, comes only from God, as a gratuitous gift. God draws near to us. From start to finish, faith remains a free and unmerited gift. But once God offers it, our response creates a relationship in which we lean on God with all our weight, that is totally, without holding back anything. Love calls forth love. This is the truth of human life. To center our lives in anything else is untruth. Genesis has described our life in the twentieth century very accurately and profoundly. Modern experience confirms the truth of the original myth.

The way one leans with all one's weight is less easy to determine. In Judeo-Christian history, one way this kind of relationship was created was through the experience of covenant. In fact, God could be described as a covenant maker. A covenant is a pact, a contract initiated by God, binding himself to us in a certain way, and us to him. In brief, God commits himself to us in a relationship of fidelity. Visible signs accompany the ratification or acceptance of these covenants and seal them as mutual commitments. In time the Old Testament experience revealed that, because God binds himself to the covenant, even if humans break it, God still remains faithful to his side and upholds his covenant forever. God was not toying with humanity. He is so serious about love that he has offered us a second chance for reconciliation. God's fidelity is a solid rock to lean upon forever. His love is everlasting; it never fades or dies.

If we return to the major covenants, God's initiation and fidelity might be more clearly exemplified. After Adam and Eve, God offers a covenant to all humanity in Noah. In the book of Genesis, when God sees that the human race has become so corrupt that nothing can straighten it out, he decides to send a flood and destroy humanity. However, one good man can still be found, so God remains faithful to his creation and offers

Noah a chance to live. Noah builds the ark in obedience to God. Noah leans on God with all his weight and is saved. God sees that the possibility of good still resides in humanity and so he makes a covenant with humanity that he will not destroy them. (This does not imply, however, that we cannot destroy ourselves in a nuclear holocaust!) A rainbow in the sky becomes the sign of that covenant. Every child knows the meaning of the rainbow: when it comes out the rain is over. The point is clear: God has committed himself to the human race and will not forsake us.

This story of Noah is a powerful statement about God's abiding love for us even in the midst of our sin. As the Noah story demonstrates, if love cannot be at the center of our lives, at least obedience can be. Obedience exists simultaneously with the theme of faith and shows what faith is in action. As the Genesis account explains, disobedience on the part of Adam and Eve (sinful action) lead to the introduction of sin. Only through obedience (correct action), done in faith, will the correct relationship with God be restored.

The second covenant is with Abraham, who is the example of the father of faith in three religions: Judaism, Islam, and Christianity. When others hear nothing but silence, Abraham hears a voice. God calls him to leave his possessions in the city of Ur and follow God into the desert, becoming a wandering nomad. Again, an act of faith. This faith leads to further tests of obedience: his wife Sarah who is barren and in old age shall conceive a son whose descendants shall be like the grains of sand on the seashore. Even though Sarah laughs in the tent when she overhears this promise of the three men, no doubt thinking they needed a biology lesson, Abraham believes the impossible. What joy and delight he takes in his son Isaac, born within the year! Then comes the apex of the obedience and act of faith: Abraham is told to take Isaac and sacrifice his life giving it back to God. We can only hear such a command as unthinkable, beyond believability. We ask what kind of God would demand this? Yes, the stakes are the highest, but we have not grasped the seriousness of belief in God, even to the point of the irrational. Abraham has: he believes and obeys. And, as we hoped but could not foresee, at the last moment God sends a messenger, an angel to stop Abraham. The point is not lost on anyone familiar with the Old Testament: as obedience becomes more difficult,

Abraham persists in faith. Or, as Adam and Eve failed in a simple command, Abraham did not fail in a more difficult one. Salvation is beginning anew. A new covenant is established, one of faith wherein God becomes related to Abraham and his descendents in a special way. Its outward sign is the symbolic act of circumcision.

God's covenant with Moses brings the first two covenants together. After the exodus, Moses goes up to the mountain where God offers a new covenant, a new relationship in which he will be their God and they his people. Obedience to the law is the outward sign. In this covenant, we see that God loves people so much that he asks for the relationships which correctly unite him with humanity. The vertical relationship between God and humanity, broken by Adam and Eve, and the horizontal relationship, broken by Cain and Abel, come together in the law. This is not law as we understand it today. This law is a precious gift whereby God reveals the secrets of the correct relationships of the world that were lost with the fall of Adam and Eve. It is a kind of return to their relationship with God in the garden. Like Adam and Eve, Moses even sees God intimately—as intimately as is then possible. Hence the reign of sin is being overcome through the law. This new covenant established the "people of Israel" and binds them to God as a people of faith. This covenant is the one Jesus is born into, lives, and uses to explain God's further covenant.

Notice that a person—or an entire people—lives within several covenants at once, each one deepening the others. Each one deepening a relationship with God. Whereas the theme of the fall is strong in theology, it is not the only interpretation of the relationship. One could just as easily say that God wants to come closer and closer to the human heart. God so loves the world that, like a passionate lover, he cannot stay away. In each covenant, God offers humanity a closer and fuller relationship to himself. Matthew, in the gospel, goes so far as to call Jesus "Emmanuel"—God with us. The history of the human race is a love story. God pursuing and wooing; ourselves pursued and wooed. It is easy to see God's activity as characteristically masculine in this activity; he is the aggressive suitor.

In the new covenant with Jesus, God further commits himself to us. Not in the law but in his spirit that dwells within us. God has now chosen to deal with us directly through the Spirit. The barrier between ourselves and God is gone forever. The law of obedience becomes the law of love, with God's spirit as the dynamic source. The Kingdom comes.

In the gospels, the obedience of Jesus as the one who both knows and does the will of the Father is the perfect attunement to God that Adam and Eve sought. The faith of Jesus is a perfect and total leaning upon God; the Son knows the heart of his Father and obeys it. Divinity and humanity unite in this love affair, and become the model of our discipleship. God promises his enduring love with Jesus' life and death, and sends his spirit who continues to dwell within us through our faith and obedience.

Hope

Because God is the faithful rock, our truth and our support, we can be sure of his constancy. This certainty of faith is the basis of Christian hope. Hope does not see what is hoped for, nor does it completely possess the object of its desire; but it does possess part of it and knows that the rest will arrive. Hope is a purchase on the future that calls for a transformation of the present. We know in faith that God will not be denied his victory.

From what we desire now because of faith—a small taste of how good these relations are now—we hope for their final completion and consummation. The theology of hope, and liberation theology as well, have emphasized the God of hope who can enter sinful situations, empower us to liberation, and bring about the Kingdom. This rediscovery of the power of hope has been an important theological contribution in recent decades. Without hope, humanity shrivels up and dies. Sin cannot be overcome. Evil wins. A God who gives us hope is a God who calls for change and transformation that we can participate in. Marx would be stunned to learn that in many places in the world a God of hope galvanizes people's involvement in society and leads the call to human dignity.

Love

Faith and hope give way to love. A God who calls us to himself, who becomes more and more involved with us, who will be faithful to us, forgives us, reconciles us, is a God who loves. A. N. Whitehead called him a "fellow sufferer who cares." While it is difficult to imagine a God with a human heart who loves as we do, it is more than true. Whatever human love is, it is "seen in a glass darkly" what God's even more immense love is for us. Human love, in other words, is an imperfect, scaled-down version of God's love. If we think we know love, we know something of God who is love. We will be even more overwhelmed by the fullness of this love when we are born again at our deaths.

This love of God is gratuitous. God did not have to love us at all, and certainly not with such passion. We can speak of a passionate God even though we know God does not have passions like we do (e.g., anger). Nevertheless, the history of salvation reveals a God who comes to us, relentlessly, without condition or warning. We can only describe such a strong love, a love that overcomes rationality and will not take "no" for an answer, as passion. The Song of Songs in the Old Testament captures the truth of God's passionate love affair with humanity. I would also like to say that there are no strings attached, that the passion is God's problem but that would be incorrect. While God does not force us, he does continue to give us the freedom to love him or not, just as he did with Adam and Eve. Hence God's passion is our problem. God wants us to accept his love and love him in return because it is best and truest for us. In brief, love is the center of human life. It is because of this truth that Jesus told us so straightforwardly what God's heart is all about: God loves us and, to paraphrase the great theologian Augustine, our hearts will be restless until they rest in loving him.

At the heart of life is not just any kind of love, but an involving love relationship with both God and neighbor. The relationship is what matters. For example, one can love without return, as a mother loves her child. The love comes first from the mother, before the child can respond. But when the child becomes an adult and loves mom back, then love becomes a reciprocal relationship. The relationship where the child is loved and loves, where mom is loved and loves, becomes the ideal. A give-and-take situation is not love. One gives and takes for the sake of the love relationship: one initiates and receives love for the sake of both people. Because we are committed to a loving relationship, each of us grows in mutual relationship with the other, both giving and receiving. One does what is best for the mutual love relationship, not for my loving or your loving. Both persons grow in the total relationship of love. One speaks, or listens, gives or takes, according to what will enhance the relationship. Not my love or your love but *our* love relationship becomes the issue. I-thou becomes we.

Faith, hope, and love are the three great theological virtues that express the one relationship with God and the forward movement of this ongoing relationship. From these, all others flow, adding dimensions of understanding to our relationship with God. For example, the virtue of justice flows from these three. Justice is not our justice but God's. Judgment about the worth of others does not come from their financial worth, status, power, or attractiveness. Justice extends to every person, even when they do not "deserve" it. The dignity of human persons is not self-evident or we would not treat people the way we do. Racism, sexism, and cultural imperialism are three cases in point: they exist, and they must be resisted. Human dignity is something that we must fight for, even when dehumanizing injustices seem more like normal fare. God calls forth a justice forged with love and not duty, right or might. The extra mile is walked, the extra tunic given, the offense pardoned even seventy times seven. One gives from one's want and not solely from one's abundance. The neighbor is loved even if he is the enemy. In other words, no border line or limiting case can be an endpoint for our loving. Justice then abounds because love abounds. The Law of an eye for an eye cannot continue; someone must blink. Right must not claim its pound of flesh. These are hard words but they are salvific words, with real power behind them. God's justice is founded upon love, and we can participate in that just love with every action.

APPENDIX FOUR: GLOSSARY

Agnosticism: The belief that it is impossible to know anything at all that is not capable of scientific description or verification. Often used to describe an openness of mind about whether God exists or not.

Aims and Objectives: Aims are broad statements of intent, expressions of the teacher's intentions, rather than what the learner should eventually be able to do. Objectives, which are measurable, are usually statements designed to identify as precisely as possible what learners should do, or be able to do, in order to demonstrate that they have learnt something.

Analogy: The comparing of two terms each of which has something in common and something different. We often express our understanding of God in analogous terms, for example, we say that The Lord is My Shepherd; the difference lies in the fact that The Lord is not a shepherd at all, while the similarity is that The Lord acts in a caring way, as shepherds do towards their flocks.

Apologetics: The study of how to defend Christianity against other ideas or world-views opposing it.

Apostles' Creed: The revised version of the oldest (fourth century ce) Christian creed, attributed by tradition to the apostles.

Atheism: The certain belief that there is no God. This is not very common because people without faith are mostly agnostics.

Babylonian Captivity: That period between the years 587 and 538 bce in which a significant number of the citizens of Jerusalem and Judea were forced to live in Babylon.

Bibliography: Description of books and other written sources providing details of authorship, title, edition and publication.

Catechesis: The process of the education in faith of the Christian, in the form of a dialogue between believers.

Catechism of the Catholic Church: A detailed and authoritative compendium of Catholic faith and teachings. It was originally published in French in 1992, with an English translation in 1994 ce.

Christ Event: A term designating Christ's coming as the decisive fact of salvation history.

Christology: The study of the nature and person of Jesus Christ and especially the relation between the divine and human in him.

Church: The community of true believers in Jesus Christ. The term is used in the New Testament both in a universal sense (all such believers) and in a particular sense (a specific group of believers in one place).

Clergy: Those who have been ordained for religious service, as distinct from the laity.

Covenant: An agreement between God and humankind in which God pledges to bless those who accept and commit themselves to Him.

Creed: A statement of what believers believe. It is used as a test of orthodoxy against unorthodox teaching.

Dei Verbum: Literally, the word of God. Also the title of the Second Vatican Council's Dogmatic Constitution on Divine Revelation (1965 ce).

Deity: A reference to God, or the possession of godhood.

Demythologising: Getting behind the mythic elements in a particular tradition.

Deutero-Isaiah: The hypothetical source of chapters 40-66 of the Book of Isaiah, which differ from the earlier half in vocabulary, style and content.

Disciple: Follower of Jesus.

Doctrine: Teaching. It can refer to the teaching of the Christian faith in general, or to a particular division of Christian teaching, for example, the doctrine of God.

Dogma: An infallible and binding religious doctrine, to be received in faith as authoritative.

Ecclesiology: The study of the Church.

Ekklesia: A Greek word used in the New Testament to describe the Church.

Epic of Gilgamesh: A Mesopotamian creation myth.

Eschatology: The study of the end of time and what lies beyond the end of time. It includes in particular the ultimate destiny and purpose of the individual human being. It is the study of the last four things: death, judgement, heaven and hell.

Essence of God: The full nature of what God is.

Exegesis: The process of expounding the original meaning of the text.

Faith: Belief in and commitment to someone or something. Christian faith is specifically a complete trust in Christ and his work as the basis of a relationship with God.

Fathers of the Church: Key thinkers and writers in the first few Christian centuries. They played a significant role in the formulation of Christian doctrine.

Fundamentalism: The belief in the infallibility and inerrancy of Sacred Scripture. It is often linked to a very literal approach to biblical interpretation.

God: In Christian theology, both a proper name and an abstract noun for deity.

Gnosticism: A varied set of religious beliefs common in the Graeco-Roman world in New Testament times. A core belief was that salvation was achieved through a secret knowledge. It saw Jesus as one as many mediators between God and humanity.

Grace: A share in God's life, an outpouring of God's goodness and generosity.

Heresy: A belief judged by the Church to be contrary to Christian tradition. It contrasts with orthodoxy.

Hermeneutics: Literally, that branch of knowledge that deals with interpretation. The study of how to interpret the Bible so that the interpretation remains faithful to the original meaning and is also relevant to contemporary culture.

Idolatry: The worship of false gods.

Immanence: God's presence within (as distinct from outside) creation. A term used to describe the nearness of God. It is usually contrasted with the Transcendence of God.

Incarnation: Literally, taking flesh. The action of God becoming wholly human in Jesus. In Jesus' humanity can be seen everything about the character of God that can be conveyed in human terms.

Inerrancy: Literally, not wandering. Freedom from error or the impossibility of making a mistake.

Kingdom of God: The reign of God.

Koinonia: The Christian fellowship of believers, with an emphasis on common religious commitment and spiritual community.

Laity: Derived from a Greek word meaning people. It is usually used to distinguish the non-ordained Christian from one who is ordained.

Liberal theology: A theology that asserts its freedom to question accepted authorities. It is often critical of orthodox Christianity.

Liturgy: The prescribed ritual for public worship. It includes the seven sacraments but is no confined to them.

Lumen Gentium: Literally, light to the nations. The title of the Second Vatican Council's Dogmatic Constitution on the Church (1964 ce).

Magisterium: The teaching authority of the Church.

Martyrology: The daily list of saints on the Church's calendar, announced each day during the liturgy of the hours in monasteries.

Metaphysical: Those things that are beyond the realm of physical observation.

Ministry: Service rendered to God and to other people.

Monotheism: The belief that there is only one God. This is a fundamental belief of Judaism, Christianity and Islam — the three great revealed religions.

Mystery: Something that we can know but never fully understand.

Natural theology: The attempt to construct a doctrine of God on the basis of reason and experience alone. There is no reference to faith or special revelation.

Natural revelation: The revelation of God as evidenced in creation. This is distinct from the special revelation of God as recorded in the Old and New Testaments.

Neo-orthodoxy: A revived orthodoxy. It emphasises that God has revealed Himself, but this revelation is not identical with the scriptures.

Omnipotence: Being all-powerful. A term usually applied to God alone.

Omnipresence: The attribute applied to God to indicate God's presence everywhere.

Omniscience: Literally, the knowing of all things. An attribute usually applied to God alone.

Ontological Argument: One of the proofs of the existence of God. The thesis is that logic demands that a being must exist who is greater than everything else. It is associated with Anselm of Canterbury.

Orthodoxy: Literally, right teaching. In Christian theology it means teaching regarded as true by the Church. It is contrasted with heresy.

Pantheism: The belief that there is no distinction between creator and creation, i.e. that all things are divine. Many pantheists worship nature.

Parameters: The boundaries, framework or guidelines of anything.

Parousia: A Greek term meaning 'coming' or 'presence'. Usually refers to the Second Coming of Christ at the end of time.

Paschal Mystery: The spiritual mystery associate with the suffering, death and resurrection of Jesus.

Patriarchy: A system of government which has all power in the hands of [the eldest] males.

Philosophy: The study of the most general principles of things and our knowledge of them.

Platonic: Influenced by Plato's philosophy — a dualism of spirit and body.

Pluralism: The belief that all religions and world-views are equally valid, and that truth claims by one imply a denigration of all others.

Polytheism: The belief that there are many gods.

Praxis: The application of Christian belief that begins with practical situations, especially those of injustice and oppression. It is a basic element of liberation theology and its hermeneutics.

Process Theology: A theology that uses becoming (as opposed to being) as the fundamental reality, and consequently is characterised as being dynamic as opposed to static.

Rationalism: A seventeenth and eighteenth century ce philosophical movement that valued reason as the final adjudicator of all statements. Rationalists often query the existence of any special revelation from God.

Rationality: Bearing the characteristic of the reasoning process, as distinct from emotions, etc.

Redemption: Literally meaning to buy back. It is used to refer to the grace of Christ who brought us back from slavery to sin. Deliverance, through divine intervention, from evil. For Christians, it is Jesus Christ as Saviour, through his sacrifice, who reconciles humanity with God and redeems us from sin.

Religion: Beliefs and practices related to a conviction that there is something higher than the individual human being.

Revelation: Literally, unveiling. God's action in making known God's self to the world.

Sacrament: An outward and visible sign of an inward and spiritual grace. It is a rite in which God's saving grace is active.

Sacramental: When the visible tangible elements of anything indicate a hidden non-tangible presence or reality.

Salvation History: A view of biblical history — originated by biblical scholars and further developed by Christian theologians — as a series of God's saving acts. Beginning with creation and ending with the Parousia. The central events are the life, death and resurrection of Jesus.

Secularism: A world-view that ignores traditional world faiths and often denies the existence of the spiritual dimension. It is characteristic of the modern western world.

Sin: Any act, attitude or disposition that fails to completely fulfil or measure up to the standards of God's righteousness. It may involve an actual transgression of God's law or failure to live up to God's norms.

Soteriology: The study of the doctrine of salvation.

Theism: The belief in one unified being which, although distinct from the cosmos, is the source of it and continues to sustain it. Theism is usually contrasted with pantheism.

Theodicy: The attempt to justify the goodness of an omnipotent God in the face of the evil and suffering seen in the world.

Theology: In its narrow sense, the study of God. In its wider sense, it includes all the subjects that comprise a programme of theological study.

Theological Anthropology: The study of human nature from the perspective of theology and revelation.

Tradition: Literally, handing over. Religious beliefs not specifically found in the Bible but considered authoritative. Tradition describes the religious teachings and practices handed down, whether in oral or written form, separately from but not independent of Scripture.

Transcendent: Something that extends beyond human and earthly concerns. An attribute often associated with God and contrasted with immanence. A quality indicating something that is beyond the grasp of reason.

Vatican II: The Second Vatican Council (1962-1965 ce). It was convened in Rome by Pope John XXIII and produced significant statements on liturgy, the Church, revelation and salvation.

Trent, Council of (1545-1563 ce): It sought to institute certain reforms in the Church and to clarify the Church's doctrines in relationship to those of the Reformers.

Yahweh: The Hebrew name of God.

THEOLOGY FOR TODAY

A DISTANCE LEARNING APPROACH TO THEOLOGY

SECTION ONE:
AN INTRODUCTION TO DISTANCE LEARNING

SECTION TWO:
INTRODUCING THEOLOGY

SECTION THREE:
REVELATION AND FAITH

The distance learning method, pioneered by the Open University, has been accepted worldwide as a flexible and accessible form of third-level education. This book guides students through the main features of this method and demonstrates the importance of the interaction between students and the module textbooks. In addition to the textbooks, this introductory book also shows how students of The Priory Institute have the additional support of launch days, local co-ordinators, study-days, tutorial days and on-line academic tutors. Theology has been described as 'faith seeking understanding'. This rational approach to faith and revelation gives students a first taste of what theology is all about.

THE PRIORY INSTITUTE

Tallaght Village, Dublin 24, Ireland
Tel: 01 4048124. Fax: 01 462 6084
Email: enquiries@prioryinstitute.com

HEALTH AND SAFETY IN KITCHENS & FOOD PREPARATION AREAS

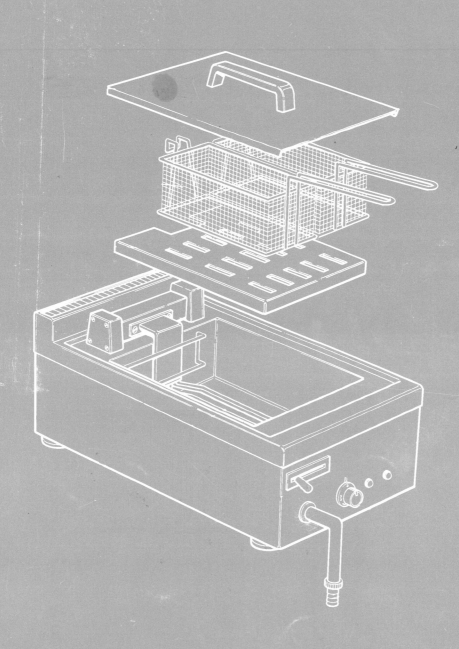